COLLEGE SERIES OF GREEK AUTHORS

EDITED UNDER THE SUPERVISION OF

JOHN WILLIAMS WHITE AND THOMAS D. SEYMOUR.

INTRODUCTION

TO THE

LANGUAGE AND VERSE

OF

HOMER

BY

THOMAS D. SEYMOUR

HILLHOUSE PROFESSOR OF GREEK IN YALE COLLEGE.

———

GINN AND COMPANY

BOSTON · NEW YORK · CHICAGO · LONDON
ATLANTA · DALLAS · COLUMBUS · SAN FRANCISCO

PREFACE.

THIS Introduction is not designed to lay stress on Homeric language as contrasted with Homeric poetry, but is intended to relieve the commentary of explanations of dialectic forms and metrical peculiarities, and to call the student's attention to the most noteworthy characteristics of Homeric style and syntax. In reading Homer, certain questions, which cannot be avoided, as to the origin and relation of forms, will attract less of the pupil's attention and demand less of the teacher's time in the class-room if the facts are stated in their proper connection; the grouping of these facts will make them more intelligible and more easily remembered.

Some peculiarities of form have not been mentioned here, since they occur so seldom that they may be treated in the commentary just as conveniently; while for divers reasons other anomalies which are no more frequent have been discussed. Nor has the author planned to make the collection of examples complete; the student should be encouraged to gather illustrations for himself.

Most of this Introduction is of a nature to be read rather than committed to memory. Much of it is unnecessary for a beginner, but the author hopes that none of it is beyond the comprehension and appreciation of the student. While parts of it can be made fully useful only by a wise teacher, most of it should be helpful to the undirected student.

YALE COLLEGE, July, 1885.

TABLE OF CONTENTS.

HOMERIC STYLE.

§ 1. a. TRANSLATIONS. Matthew Arnold enumerates four essential characteristics of Homer's poetry:[1] "Homer is rapid in his movement, Homer is plain in his words and style, Homer is simple in his ideas, Homer is noble in his manner. Cowper renders him ill because he is slow in his movement and elaborate in his style; Pope renders him ill because he is artificial both in his style and in his words; Chapman renders him ill because he is fantastic in his ideas; Mr. Newman renders him ill because he is odd in his words and ignoble in his manner." Or in other words: "Between Cowper and Homer there is interposed the mist of Cowper's elaborate Miltonic manner, entirely alien to the flowing rapidity of Homer; between Pope and Homer there is interposed the mist of Pope's literary, artificial manner, entirely alien to the plain naturalness of Homer's manner; between Chapman and Homer there is interposed the mist of the fancifulness of the Elizabethan age, entirely alien to the plain directness of Homer's thought and feeling; while between Mr. Newman and Homer is interposed a cloud of more than Egyptian thickness, — namely, a manner, in Mr. Newman's version eminently ignoble, while Homer's manner is eminently noble."

If poets and masters have thus failed, it is evident that it is no easy achievement to translate Homer well, to be at the same time rapid, plain, simple, and noble, — οὔ πως ἅμα

---

[1] *Essays in Criticism*, Boston, 1865, pp. 284 ff., or *Studies in Celtic Literature and on Translating Homer*, Macmillan, N.Y., 1883, pp. 138 ff.

πάντα δυνήσεαι αὐτὸς ἑλέσθαι. The beginner can at least be
simple ; he should aim to attain the other qualities also.

It is instructive to compare different translations of a
famous passage, Θ 555 ff. : —

> ὡς δ' ὅτ' ἐν οὐρανῷ ἄστρα φαεινὴν ἀμφὶ σελήνην
> φαίνετ' ἀριπρεπέα, ὅτε τ' ἔπλετο νήνεμος αἰθήρ·
> ἔκ τ' ἔφανεν πᾶσαι σκοπιαὶ καὶ πρώονες ἄκροι
> καὶ νάπαι· οὐρανόθεν δ' ἄρ' ὑπερράγη ἄσπετος αἰθήρ,
> πάντα δέ τ' εἴδεται ἄστρα· γέγηθε δέ τε φρένα ποιμήν·
> τόσσα μεσηγὺ νεῶν ἠδὲ Ξάνθοιο ῥοάων
> Τρώων καιόντων πυρὰ φαίνετο Ἰλιόθι πρό.
> χίλι' ἄρ' ἐν πεδίῳ πυρὰ καίετο, πὰρ δὲ ἑκάστῳ
> εἵατο πεντήκοντα σέλαι πυρὸς αἰθομένοιο.
> ἵπποι δὲ κρῖ λευκὸν ἐρεπτόμενοι καὶ ὀλύρας,
> ἑσταότες παρ' ὄχεσφιν, ἐΰθρονον Ἠῶ μίμνον.

This is translated by Chapman : [1] —

[1] *The Iliads of Homer, Prince of Poets, never before in any language truly
translated, with a comment upon some of his chief places, done according to the
Greek by George Chapman.* Of this translation, A–B, H–Λ were published in
1598. The first twelve books of the Iliad were published in 1610, and the
other twelve in 1611. The first half of the Odyssey was published in 1614, and
the rest in 1615. Chapman was about six years older than Shakespeare. The
reader will notice that the metre is the "common metre" of our hymn-books.

Chapman says in his "Preface to the Reader" : "Alwaies conceiving how
pedanticall and absurd an affectation it is, in the interpretation of any Author
(much more of *Homer*) to turn him word for word ; when (according to *Horace*
and other best lawgivers to translators) it is the part of every knowing and
judiciall interpreter, not to follow the number and order of the words but the
material things themselves, and sentences to weigh diligently ; and to clothe
and adorne them with words, and such a stile and form of oration as are most
apt for the language into which they are converted. If I have not turned
him in any place falsly (as all other his interpreters have in many, and most
of his chiefe places ;) if I have not left behind me any of his sentence, ele-
gancie, height, intention and invention : if in some few places . . . I be somthing
paraphrasticall and faulty ; is it justice in that poore fault (if they will needs
have it so) to drowne all the rest of my labour."

Pope criticises Chapman's translation as "loose and rambling," and for its
"frequent interpolations." "He appears to have had a strong affectation of
extracting new meanings out of his author. . . . But that which is to be allowed
him, and which very much contributed to cover his defects, is a daring, fiery

" Fires round about them shinde
As when about the silver Moone, when air is free from winde,
And stars shine cleare ; to whose sweete beames, high prospects,
    and the brows
Of all steepe hils and pinnacles, thrust up themselves for showes ;
And even the lowly vallies joy, to glitter in their sight,
When the unmeasur'd firmament, bursts to disclose her light,
And all the signes in heaven are seene, that glad the shepheards
    hart ;
So many fires disclosde their beames, made by the Trojan part,
Before the face of *Ilion ;* and her bright turrets show'd.
A thousand courts of guard kept fires ; and every guard allow'd
Fiftie stout men, by whom their horse, eate oates and hard white
    corne,
And all did wilfully expect, the silver-throned morne."

Pope's translation[1] follows : —

" And beaming fires illumin'd all the ground,
    As when the moon, refulgent lamp of night !
O'er heaven's clear azure spreads her sacred light,
    When not a breath disturbs the deep serene,

spirit that animates his translation, which is something like what one might
imagine Homer himself would have writ before he arriv'd to years of discretion."

[1] Pope's translation of the Iliad was published in 1715-20. It is said that
the great Bentley (see § 14 *d* R.) remarked to Pope "that it was a very
pretty poem but that he must not call it Homer." It is in such simple narrative as quoted above that Pope's style is worst ; it is best in descriptions of
action.

Pope says in his preface : "That which in my opinion ought to be the
endeavour of any one who translates Homer, is above all things to keep alive
that spirit and fire which makes his chief character. In particular places,
where the sense can bear any doubt, to follow the strongest and most poetical,
as most agreeing with that character. To copy him in all the variations of
his style and the different modulations of his numbers. To preserve in the
more active or more descriptive parts, a warmth and elevation ; in the more
sedate or narrative, a plainness and solemnity ; in the speeches, a fulness and
perspicuity ; in the sentences [*sententiae*], a shortness and gravity. Not to
neglect even the little figures and turns on the words, nor sometimes the very
cast of the periods. Neither to omit or confound any rites or customs of
antiquity. . . . To consider him attentively in comparison with Virgil above
all the ancients, and with Milton above all the moderns."

And not a cloud o'ercasts the solemn scene ;
Around her throne the vivid planets roll,
And stars unnumber'd gild the glowing pole,
O'er the dark trees a yellow verdure shed,
And tip with silver every mountain's head ;
Then shine the vales, the rocks in prospect rise,
A flood of glory bursts from all the skies :
The conscious swains, rejoicing in the sight,
Eye the blue vault and bless the useful light.
So many flames before proud Ilion blaze,
And lighten glimmering Xanthus with their rays :
The long reflections of the distant fires
Gleam on the walls, and tremble on the spires,
A thousand piles the dusky horrors gild,
And shoot a shady lustre o'er the field.
Full fifty guards each flaming pile attend,
Whose umber'd arms, by fits, thick flashes send,
Loud neigh the coursers o'er the heaps of corn,
And ardent warriors wait the rising morn."

Cowper's translation [1] follows : —

" As when about the clear bright moon, the stars
Shine in full splendour, and the winds are hush'd,
The groves, the mountain-tops, the headland-heights
Stand all apparent, not a vapour streaks

---

[1] Published in 1791.

Cowper says in his preface : "My chief boast is that I have adhered closely
to the original, convinced that every departure from him would be punished
with the forfeiture of some grace or beauty for which I could offer no sub-
stitute. . . . It has been my point everywhere to be as little verbose as possible.
. . . In the affair of style, I have endeavoured neither to creep nor to bluster,
for no author is so likely to betray his translator into both these faults as
Homer, though himself never guilty of either. . . . The passages which will be
least noticed . . . are those which have cost me abundantly the most labour.
It is difficult to kill a sheep with dignity in a modern language, to flay and to
prepare it for the table, detailing every circumstance of the process. Difficult
also, without sinking below the level of poetry, to harness mules to a waggon,
particularizing every article of their furniture, straps, rings, staples, and even
the tying of the knots that kept all together. Homer, who writes always to
the eye, with all his sublimity and grandeur, has the minuteness of a Flemish
painter."

> The boundless blue, but ether open'd wide
> All glitters and the shepherd's heart is cheer'd;
> So num'rous seem'd those fires between the stream
> Of Xanthus, blazing, and the fleet of Greece,
> In prospect all of Troy; a thousand fires,
> Each watch'd by fifty warriors seated near.
> The steeds beside the chariots stood, their corn
> Chewing, and waiting till the golden thron'd
> Aurora should restore the light of day."

Professor F. W. Newman's translation [1] follows:—

> " And as around the shining Moon | the stars aloft in heaven
> Glister with radiance distinct, | when all the sky is breathless,
> And every lofty peak is shown, | and headland edge and forest,
> And from behind the cloven sky | unfathom'd heaven gleameth;
> Nor hidden any star may be; | and joyful is the shepherd;
> So many fires betwixt the streams | of Xanthos and the galleys,
> Shone then in front of Ilion, | by hands of Troians kindled.
> A thousand fires along the plain, | I say, that night were burning,
> And close to every glaring blaze | sat fifty men in armour.
> And by their chariots the steeds | rye and white barley munching,
> Stood waiting till the Queen of Morn | fair-thron'd should rise
>   before them."

Lord Derby's translation [2] follows:—

> " As when in Heav'n, around the glitt'ring moon
> The stars shine bright amid the breathless air;
> And ev'ry crag and ev'ry jutting peak

[1] Published in 1856.

This has received perhaps undue distinction from the criticisms of Matthew Arnold. The translator says: "To the metre which I have myself adopted, I was brought by a series of argument and experiment, and was afterwards gratified to find that I had exactly alighted on the modern Greek Epic metre. It is also the metre of the American Yankee Doodle, which some have ignorantly made an objection: as if the metre of the *Frogs and Mice* and of the *Margites*, were not that of the *Iliad*. Of course no metre can be popular, without being applicable to low treatment; indeed without being liable to degenerate into doggrel in unskilful hands."

[2] Published in 1865.

Stands boldly forth, and ev'ry forest glade ;
Ev'n to the gates of Heav'n is open'd wide
The boundless sky ; shines each particular star
Distinct ; joy fills the gazing shepherd's heart.
So bright, so thickly scatter'd o'er the plain,
Before the walls of Troy, between the ships
And Xanthus' stream, the Trojan watchfires blaz'd.
    A thousand fires burnt brightly ; and round each
Sat fifty warriors in the ruddy glare ;
With store of provender before them laid,
Barley and rye, the tether'd horses stood
Beside the cars, and waited for the morn."

Bryant's translation [1] follows : —

" As when in heaven the stars look brightly forth
Round the clear-shining moon, while not a breeze
Stirs in the depths of air, and all the stars
Are seen, and gladness fills the shepherd's heart,
So many fires in sight of Ilium blazed,
Lit by the sons of Troy, between the ships
And eddying Xanthus : on the plain there shone
A thousand ; fifty warriors by each fire
Sat in its light.   Their steeds beside the cars —
Champing their oats and their white barley — stood,
And waited for the golden morn to rise."

Tennyson translates : —

" As when in heaven the stars about the moon
Look beautiful, when all the winds are laid,
And every height comes out, and jutting peak
And valley, and the immeasurable heavens
Break open to their highest, and all the stars
Shine, and the shepherd gladdens in his heart :
So many a fire between the ships and stream
Of Xanthus blazed before the towers of Troy,
A thousand on the plain ; and close by each

[1] Published in 1870.

Sat fifty in the blaze of burning fire ;
And champing golden grain, the horses stood
Hard by their chariots, waiting for the dawn."

Matthew Arnold translates the last verses in hexameters : —

" So shone forth, in front of Troy, by the bed of the Xanthus,
Between that and the ships, the Trojans' numerous fires.
In the plain there were kindled a thousand fires : by each one
There sat fifty men in the ruddy light of the fire :
By their chariots stood the steeds and champed the white barley
While their masters sat by the fire and waited for Morning."

b. CHANGE OF SUBJECT. Homer composed for quick-
minded hearers, who were ready to apprehend a change of
subject even when it was marked by no pronoun, as ἥ οἱ ἅμ'
αἰθομένας δαΐδας φέρε καί ἑ μάλιστα | δμωάων φιλέεσκε, καὶ
ἔτρεφε τύτθον ἐόντα a 434 f. *she bore for him the burning
torch and (i.e. for) he loved her most of all the female ser-
vants, and (i.e. for) she was his nurse when he was a child;*
ἔχεν πάλαι ὡς ἴθυνεν Ψ 871 *he* (Meriones) *long had been hold-
ing while he* (Teucer) *was taking aim;* πρίν γ' ἠὲ κατακτάμεν
ἠὲ κατ' ἄκρης | Ἴλιον αἰπεινὴν ἐλέειν κτάσθαι τε πολίτας
Ο 557 *before either* we *slay* the Greeks *or* they *capture
lofty Ilios and the citizens are slain.* Still more striking is
the change in βουλοίμην κε . . τεθνάμεν ἢ τάδε . . ἔργ' ὁρά-
ασθαι, | ξείνους τε στυφελιζομένους δμῳάς τε γυναῖκας | ῥυστά-
ζοντας ἀεικελίως κατὰ δώματα καλά, | καὶ οἶνον διαφυσσόμενον,
καὶ σῖτον ἔδοντας π 106 ff. *I should rather die than see these
deeds, — guests struck,* suitors *abusing the maids, wine wasted,*
suitors *devouring the food,* where the poet was sure that his
hearers would not construe ῥυστάζοντας and ἔδοντας with
ξείνους, but would supply μνηστῆρας from the context.

c. DIRECT DISCOURSE. Like the writers of Holy Scrip-
ture, and as in the simple style of ballads and fairy tales and
the conversation of children and uneducated persons, the
Homeric poet avoids the use of *indirect discourse ;* he has no

long passages in *oratio obliqua*, in the manner of the reported
speeches in Caesar's Commentaries.   He passes quickly from
indirect to direct discourse,[1] as ἐπεὶ πρό οἱ εἴπομεν ἡμεῖς |
μήτ' αὐτὸν κτείνειν μήτε μνάασθαι ἄκοιτιν, | ἐκ γὰρ Ὀρέσταο
τίσις ἔσσεται κτλ. a 37 ff. *since we told him beforehand not to
slay the man himself and not to woo his wife, for from Orestes
shall* (for *should*) *vengeance come, etc.*   Contrast ὁ γὰρ ἦλθε
θοὰς ἐπὶ νῆας Ἀχαιῶν | . . καὶ λίσσετο πάντας Ἀχαιοὺς |
. . ὑμῖν μὲν θεοὶ δοῖεν Ὀλύμπια δώματ' ἔχοντες | ἐκπέρσαι
Πριάμοιο πόλιν, εὖ δ' οἴκαδ' ἱκέσθαι· | παῖδα δ' ἐμοὶ λύσαιτε
φίλην τὰ δ' ἄποινα δέχεσθαι, | ἁζόμενοι Διὸς υἱόν, ἑκηβόλον
Ἀπόλλωνα A 12 ff. with its paraphrase which uses indirect
discourse, ἐλθὼν·ὁ ἱερεὺς εὔχετο ἐκείνοις μὲν τοὺς θεοὺς δοῦναι
ἑλόντας τὴν Τροίαν αὐτοὺς σωθῆναι, τὴν δὲ θυγατέρα οἱ λῦσαι
δεξαμένους ἄποινα καὶ τὸν θεὸν αἰδεσθέντας κτλ. in Plato *Rep.*
III 393 E.

d. PRINCIPAL CLAUSES.   Similar to this avoidance of
indirect discourse is the poet's frequent and ready transition
from a subordinate to a principal clause, as ὃς μέγα πάντων |
Ἀργείων κρατέει καί οἱ πείθονται Ἀχαιοί A 78 f. *who rules
with might over all the Argives and him* (for *whom*) *the
Achaeans obey;* ὃς μάλα πολλὰ | πλάγχθη . . πολλὰ δ' ὅ γ'
ἐν πόντῳ πάθεν ἄλγεα a 1 ff. *who was driven on many wander-
ings . . and he suffered many woes upon the sea;* Μέντωρ ὅς
ῥ' Ὀδυσῆος ἀμύμονος ἦεν ἑταῖρος | καί οἱ (Mentor) ἰὼν ἐν νηυ-
σὶν ἐπέτρεπεν (sc. Odysseus) οἶκον ἄπαντα β 225 f., ᾧ ἔπι
πολλὰ μόγησα, δόσαν δέ μοι υἷες Ἀχαιῶν A 162.

e. Thus the poet deserts the participial for a finite construc-
tion, as Ἕκτορα δ' ἐν πεδίῳ ἴδε κείμενον· ἀμφὶ δ' ἑταῖροι | εἴατο
O 9 f. *he saw Hector lying on the plain, while his comrades were*

---

[1] So in other early poets as ἦρε' ὅττι δηὖτε πέπονθα, κὄττι | δηὖτε κάλημι, |
κὄττι μοι μάλιστα θέλω γενέσθαι | μαινόλᾳ θύμῳ· τίνα δηὖτε Πείθω | μαῖς ἄγην ἐς
σὰν φιλότατα, τίς σ' ὦ | Ψάπφ' ἀδικήει; Sappho 1 15 ff. *thou didst ask me what I
suffer and why I call thee, . . whom dost thou desire that Persuasion should lead
to thy love, etc.*

seated around him (for καὶ ἑταίρους ἡμένους) ; μνηστῆρες ἠγε-
ρέθοντο | ἔσθλ᾽ ἀγορεύοντες, κακὰ δὲ φρεσὶ βυσσοδόμευον ρ 65 f.
(for βυσσοδομεύοντες *planning in the depth of their hearts*).
Cf. γουνάζομαι . . | ἑστάμεναι κρατερῶς, μηδὲ τρωπᾶσθε φό-
βονδε Ο 665 f. *I beseech you to stand stoutly, nor turn to flight;*
ἰοῖσίν τε τιτυσκόμενοι λάεσσί τ᾽ ἔβαλλον Γ 80, where τέ . . τέ
mark the imperfect as correlative with the participle.

f. ORDER OF WORDS. The simplicity of the Homeric
order of words is most clearly seen by comparing a passage
of Homer with a similar passage of a later Greek poet or of
Vergil. Many verses of the Iliad and Odyssey can be translated into English, word for word as they stand, as ᾠχόμεθ᾽
ἐς Θήβην ἱερὴν πόλιν Ἠετίωνος, | τὴν δὲ διεπράθομέν τε καὶ
ἤγομεν ἐνθάδε πάντα. | . . ἐκ δ᾽ ἕλον Ἀτρείδῃ Χρυσηίδα καλλι-
πάρῃον κτλ. Α 366 ff. When the order differs essentially
from the English there are generally rhetorical or poetical
reasons why the order is what it is; no one should suppose
that the metre compelled the poet to adopt an arrangement
of words that was not natural and did not please him. The
verse gave prominence not merely to the first word but often
to the word before the principal caesural pause (§ 40).

g. The thought of each Homeric verse is somewhat more
independent than is the case in later poetry. Other things
being equal, a word should be construed with words in the
same rather than in another verse. Rarely does a descriptive
adjective at the close of one verse agree directly with a noun
at the beginning of the next (as χρεμέτιζον ἐπ᾽ ἄκρῳ | χείλει
ἐφεσταότες Μ 51 f. or εἵλετο καλὴν | ἀξίνην εὔχαλκον Ν 611).

h. A noun at the close of one verse often has an adjective
apparently in agreement with it at the beginning of the next
verse, but this adjective may be regarded as in apposition
with the noun; it frequently serves to form a closer connec-
tion with a following amplifying clause, as μῆνιν ἄειδε θεά . . |
οὐλομένην, ἣ μυρί᾽ Ἀχαιοῖς ἄλγε᾽ ἔθηκεν Α 1 f., where the relative clause explains οὐλομένην: the *wrath* was *mortal, deadly,*

because it brought ten thousand woes upon the Achaeans.
So a few verses later, νοῦσον ἀνὰ στρατὸν ὦρσε κακήν, ὀλέκοντο
δὲ λαοί A 10, the position of the adjective κακήν is explained
by its connection with the thought of the following clause.
Cf. νήπιοι οἳ κατὰ βοῦς Ὑπερίονος ἠελίοιο | ἤσθιον a 8, the
companions of Odysseus were fools in that they devoured the
cattle of Hyperion; φάτις .. | ἐσθλή, χαίρουσιν δὲ πατὴρ καὶ
πότνια μήτηρ ζ 30; νῦν αὖτέ μιν υἶες Ἀχαιῶν | ἐν παλάμῃς
φορέουσι δικασπόλοι οἵ τε θέμιστας | πρὸς Διὸς εἰρύαται
A 237 ff., where δικασπόλοι is explained by the following
clause. Sometimes a word is reserved for the beginning of a
verse in order to mark a contrast with what follows, as αὐτὰρ
ἐπεὶ δὴ τεῖχος ἐπεσσυμένους ἐνόησεν | Τρῶας, ἀτὰρ Δαναῶν
γένετο ἰαχή τε φόβος τε O 395 f., where the order of the
words sets Τρῶας into an antithesis with Δαναῶν, — ἀμφοτέ-
ρας .. χεῖρας ἔμαρπτεν | σκαιῇ, δεξιτερῇ δ᾽ ἄρ᾽ ἀπ᾽ ὤμων αἴνυτο
τόξα Φ 489 f. αὐτόν thus often contrasts a man with his
companions or possessions, as ἀπὸ μὲν φίλα εἵματα δύσω |
αὐτὸν δὲ κλαίοντα θοὰς ἐπὶ νῆας ἀφήσω B 261 ff.; ἔγχος μέν ῥ᾽
ἔστησε .. | αὐτὴν δ᾽ ἐς θρόνον εἷσεν a 127 ff.

i. The first words of successive verses occasionally carry
the burden of thought, as Γλαῦκος .. | Ἰφίνοον βάλε .. | Δεξιά-
δην .. | ὦμον H 13 ff. *Glaucus .. hit Iphinous .. son of Dexias
on the shoulder.*

j. The subject of the sentence usually precedes its verb.
Almost every exception to this remark is found either at the
close of the verse, or less frequently before the principal
caesura (where the same metrical freedom was allowed as at
the end of the verse, § 41 *a* 3).

k. In order to give prominence to an important word, it is
sometimes placed before the relative word of the clause to
which it belongs, as σαώτερος ὥς κε νέηαι A 32; κεῖθι δέ μ᾽
ὡς περάσειε ξ 297. This is especially frequent when the subordinate clause precedes the principal sentence, as Ἕκτωρ δ᾽
ὡς Σκαιάς τε πύλας .. ἵκανεν | ἀμφ᾽ ἄρα μιν .. θέον κτλ. Z 237.

l. Adnominal genitives, like adjectives, generally precede
their noun, except at the close of the verse or before a caesural pause, but there are many exceptions to the rule in the
case of adjectives, principally perhaps where the adjective
and substantive are closely connected. A preposition often
stands between the adjective and noun, as χρυσέῳ ἀνὰ σκή-
πτρῳ Α 15, θοὰς ἐπὶ νῆας Α 12; ἡμετέρῳ ἐνὶ οἴκῳ Α 30; or
νῆας ἔπι γλαφυράς Γ 119. The infinitive generally follows
the verb on which it depends.

m. When a noun is modified by two adjectives, it frequently is preceded by one and followed by the other, as θοῇ
παρὰ νηὶ μελαίνῃ Α 300; πολὺν ὄμβρον ἀθέσφατον Κ 6. So
in English poetry "human face divine," "purest ray serene,"
"old man eloquent."

n. EPITHETS. Often three or more epithets are used with
one noun, as εἵλετο δ᾽ ἄλκιμον ἔγχος ἀκαχμένον ὀξέϊ χαλκῷ, |
βριθὺ μέγα στιβαρόν α 99 f.; οὔ τι περιπληθὴς λίην τόσον,
ἀλλ᾽ ἀγαθὴ μέν, | εὔβοτος εὔμηλος, οἰνοπληθὴς πολύπυρος
ο 405 f. (But in the first three books of the Iliad as many
as three adjectives are rarely found with one noun.) Often
two of the epithets begin a verse, as ἐς θρόνον εἷσεν ἄγων . . |
καλὸν δαιδάλεον α 130 f.; φόρμιγγι λιγείῃ | καλῇ δαιδαλέῃ
Ι 186 f.; καλὰ πέδιλα | ἀμβρόσια χρύσεια ε 44 f.; ἐς θάλα-
μον κατεβήσετο κηώεντα | κέδρινον ὑψόροφον Ω 191 f.

o. As is seen from the foregoing examples, the poet does
not use καί to connect *epitheta ornantia*.

p. These ornamental epithets frequently have reference to
the most marked natural characteristics of an object rather
than to a particular occasion. The ships are *swift* (*θοαί*)
even when they are drawn up on land (Α 300 and *passim*);
clothing is σιγαλόεντα even when it is soiled (ζ 26); Aegis-
thus is called *honorable, blameless* (ἀμύμων, α 29) in the very
breath in which he is rebuked for wooing Agamemnon's wife
and killing the king of men himself; Polyphemus lifts his
hands to the starry heaven (εἰς οὐρανὸν ἀστερόεντα ι 527) in

broad daylight. The sea is πολύφλοισβος, ἠχήεσσα, εὐρύπορος, ἀτρύγετος, ἀθέσφατος, πολιή, γλαυκή. Rarely would one of these epithets be used to give a characteristic of the sea at a special time. It is in imitation of Homer that Theocritus, *Id.* I 58, calls milk λευκόν, — of course, not to distinguish white milk from milk of another color but to bring the object vividly before the mind by mentioning a quality of it which all would recognize as belonging to the nature of the object. The choice among these stereotyped conventional epithets was often determined by the convenience of metre or rhythm (see § 4 *b* f.). It should be noted that of the epithets of the sea only two (ἀτρύγετος, εὐρύπορος) have the same metrical value.

q. Almost every prominent person in the poems has some special epithet or epithets. Pope calls these "a sort of supernumerary pictures of the persons or things they are joined to. We see the motion of Hector's plumes in the epithet κορυθαίολος." No one but Athena is γλαυκῶπις and the adjective becomes virtually a proper name, as γ 135. She bears this epithet 90 times, generally in the phrase θεὰ γλαυκῶπις Ἀθήνη. She is Παλλὰς Ἀθήνη 41 times. Zeus is νεφεληγερέτα Ζεύς 30 times, ἐρίγδουπος πόσις Ἥρης 7 times, εὐρύοπα Ζεύς 20 times, μητίετα Ζεύς 19 times, αἰγίοχος (generally in the genitive, αἰγιόχοιο) 54 times, πατὴρ ἀνδρῶν τε θεῶν τε 15 times. Poseidon is γαιήοχος ἐννοσίγαιος 8 times, Ποσειδάων ἐνοσίχθων 24 times. Hera with a few mortal women shares the by-name λευκώλενος (24 times, generally in the phrase θεὰ λευκώλενος Ἥρη), and she is βοῶπις πότνια Ἥρη 14 times. The Achaeans are ἐυκνήμιδες Ἀχαιοί 36 times, κάρη κομόωντες 29 times, in the genitive Ἀχαιῶν χαλκοχιτώνων 24 times, υἷες Ἀχαιῶν 64 times, λαὸς Ἀχαιῶν 22 times, κοῦροι Ἀχαιῶν 9 times. Agamemnon is ἄναξ ἀνδρῶν forty-five times in the Iliad and thrice in the Odyssey, while this title is given to only five other chiefs, once to each. Achilles is ποδάρκης δῖος Ἀχιλλεύς 21 times, πόδας ὠκὺς Ἀχιλλεύς 30 times,

ποδώκεος Αἰακίδαο 10 times, ποδώκεα Πηλείωνα 10 times.
Odysseus is πολύτλας δῖος Ὀδυσσεύς 42 times, πολύμητις
Ὀδυσσεύς 78 times, Ὀδυσσῆος θείοιο 27 times, Λαερτιάδεω
Ὀδυσῆος 11 times, πολυμήχαν᾽ Ὀδυσσεῦ 24 times. Iris, the
messenger of the gods in the Iliad, is ποδήνεμος ὠκέα Ἶρις
9 times. Hector is κορυθαίολος 37 times, φαίδιμος Ἕκτωρ
30 times. *Cf.* 'pius Aeneas,' 'fidus Achates.'

r. The situation of the moment seems sometimes to con-
tradict the epithet, as τὸν δὲ ἰδὼν ῥίγησε βοὴν ἀγαθὸς Διομήδης
Ε 596 *at sight of him Diomed good at the war cry shuddered.*

s. SYNONYMOUS EXPRESSIONS. The poet is fond of a
cumulation of synonymous or nearly synonymous expressions, many of which remind the reader of redundant legal
expressions, as φωνήσας προσηύδα Α 201 *lifted up his voice
and addressed her;* ἔπος τ᾽ ἔφατ᾽ ἔκ τ᾽ ὀνόμαζεν Α 361 *spoke
a word and called upon him;* ἐμεῦ ζῶντος καὶ ἐπὶ χθονὶ
δερκομένοιο Α 88; ἀπριάτην ἀνάποινον Α 99, τῶν οὔ τι μετατρέπῃ οὐδ᾽ ἀλεγίζεις Α 160, πόλεμοί τε μάχαι τε Α 177, πάντων
μὲν κρατέειν ἐθέλει πάντεσσι δ᾽ ἀνάσσειν, | πᾶσι δὲ σημαίνειν
Α 288 f., οὔτ᾽ εἴρομαι οὔτε μεταλλῶ Α 553, ὄψεαι εἴ κ᾽ ἐθέλησθα
καὶ εἴ κέν τοι τὰ μεμήλῃ Δ 353, ἡγήτορες ἠδὲ μέδοντες Β 79,
ἄβρομοι αὐίαχοι Ν 41, ὄλβῳ τε πλούτῳ τε Ω 536, ἄιστος
ἄπυστος a 242, νηπενθές τ᾽ ἄχολόν τε δ 221, ἀρρήκτους ἀλύτους
θ 275. Sometimes the same stem is repeated for emphasis,
in a different form, as ὄψιμον ὀψιτέλεστον Β 325, κεῖτο μέγας
μεγαλωστί Σ 26, ἀπώλετο λυγρῷ ὀλέθρῳ γ 87.

t. EPEXEGESIS. A clause is often added epexegetically,
to explain a preceding clause or word, as νημερτέα βουλήν, |
νόστον Ὀδυσσῆος ταλασίφρονος, ὥς κε νέηται a 86 f., where
νόστον is in apposition with βουλήν and is itself explained
by ὥς κε νέηται, — πατροφονῆα . . ὅ οἱ πατέρα κλυτὸν ἔκτα
a 299 f.; μῆνιν . . οὐλομένην ἣ μυρί᾽ Ἀχαιοῖς ἄλγε᾽ ἔθηκεν
Α 1 f.; τεῖχος ἄρειον ὅ κ᾽ ἀνδράσι λοιγὸν ἀμῦναι Ο 736 *a better
wall* (namely, one) *which would ward off destruction from the
men;* γιγνομένῳ . . ὅτε μιν τέκε μήτηρ η 198; τά τε δῶρ᾽ Ἀφρο-

δίτης, | ἥ τε κόμη τό τε εἶδος Γ 54 f.; ἀρετὴν σὴν φαινέμεν ἤ
τοι ὀπηδεῖ θ 237; εἰ μὲν δὴ νῦν τοῦτο φίλον μακάρεσσι θεοῖ-
σιν, | νοστῆσαι Ὀδυσῆα πολύφρονα ὅνδε δόμονδε κτλ. a 82.
For explanatory asyndeton, see § 2 *m*.

u. The species often follows in apposition with the genus,
as κύματα μακρὰ θαλάσσης | πόντου Ἰκαρίοιο Β 144 f.; ἴρηξ |
κίρκος ν 86 f.; βοῦς | ταῦρος Β 480 f.; συὸς κάπρου Ρ 21; ὄρνι-
σιν αἰγυπιοῖσιν Η 59. *Cf.* ἔκτοθεν ἄλλων | μνηστήρων a 132 f.
apart from the others, the suitors, and the epexegetical use of
the infinitive, as ἔριδι ξυνέηκε μάχεσθαι Α 8 *brought together
in strife, to contend.*

v. Thus also the part of the mind or body which is employed or especially affected is mentioned, as οὐκ Ἀγαμέμνονι
ἥνδανε θυμῷ Α 24, χωόμενος κῆρ Α 44, κεχαροίατο θυμῷ Α 256,
ἐν ὀφθαλμοῖσιν ὁρᾶσθαι Γ 306, ποσὶ προβιβάς Ν 158, πάθεν
ἄλγεα ὃν κατὰ θυμόν a 4.

w. STEREOTYPED EXPRESSIONS. The same expressions
recur under similar circumstances. We find a stereotyped
description of a feast and of the preparations for it, of the
breaking of day and of the approach of night, of doffing or
donning sandals and armor; there are conventional expressions
for setting out on a journey, for an attack in battle, for the fall
and death of a warrior, for lying down to rest. Speeches are
introduced and followed by set verses, as καί μιν (or σφεας)
φωνήσας ἔπεα πτερόεντα προσηύδα Α 201, and in fifty other
places; ὅ σφιν ἐὺ φρονέων ἀγορήσατο καὶ μετέειπεν Α 73 and
in fourteen other places, while the second hemistich is found
several times in other combinations; ἦ τοι ὅ γ᾽ ὣς εἰπὼν κατ᾽
ἄρ᾽ ἕζετο, τοῖσι δ᾽ ἀνέστη Α 68, 101, Β 76, Η 354, 365, β 224.
These stereotyped verses have been compared with the frequently recurring " And Job answered and said," " Then
Eliphaz the Temanite answered and said," of the book of
Job, and with the set form in which the reports of the mes-
sengers were brought to the man of Uz, — each of the four
reports ending "and I only am escaped alone to tell thee."

§ 2. a. PARECHESIS, ONOMATOPOEIA, *etc.* The poet seems
to have looked with indifference on the similarity of sound
in neighboring words. He does not appear to have designed
the rhyme in ἱκέσθαι, δέχεσθαι Α 19 f., δώσει, ἀπώσει Α 96 f.,
χέουσα, τεκοῦσα Α 413 f., ἔρυσσαν, τάνυσσαν Α 485 f., or in
instances like Ξ 9 ff., where three successive verses rhyme,
ending ἑοῖο, ἱπποδάμοιο, ἑοῖο, or between the two hemistichs
of a verse, as ἔσπετε νῦν μοι Μοῦσαι Ὀλύμπια δώματ' ἔχουσαι Β 484.

Most examples of parechesis (παρήχησις) and alliteration
are probably accidental, as πολλέων ἐκ πολίων Β 131, ἐς πόλε-
μον πωλήσεαι Ε 350, κεῖνός γε ἐοικότι κεῖται α 46, ἀμφ' Ὀδυσῆι
δαΐφρονι δαίεται ἦτορ α 48, δασσάμενοι δαίνυντ' ἐρικυδέα δαῖτα
γ 66, πατρί τε σῷ μέγα πῆμα πόληΐ τε παντί τε δήμῳ Γ 50.

b. Occasionally an onomatopoetic (ὀνοματοποιία), imitative
expression is used, giving a kind of echo in the sound, as
τριχθά τε καὶ τετραχθά Γ 363, of the breaking of the sword
of Menelaus; πολλὰ δ' ἄναντα κάταντα πάραντά τε δόχμιά
τ' ἦλθον Ψ 116, of the men and mules going up hill and
down, over a rough road for wood; ἐκ δὲ Χρυσηὶς νηὸς βῆ
ποντοπόροιο Α 439, where a vivid imagination may perhaps
hear the measured steps of the damsel as she leaves the ship,
with a quick rush at the close; κύματα παφλάζοντα πολυ-
φλοίσβοιο θαλάσσης Ν 798; αὖτις ἔπειτα πέδονδε κυλίνδετο
λᾶας ἀναιδής λ 598, of the rolling back of the stone which
Sisyphus in Hades was continually urging to the summit of
a hill.

c. The poet plays occasionally on the names of his heroes,
as Πρόθοος θοὸς ἡγεμόνευεν Β 758 ("swift by nature as well as
by name"); Τληπόλεμον . . . τλήμονα θυμὸν ἔχων Ε 668 ff.;
Εὐπείθει πείθοντο ω 465 f.; Ἕκτορ . . φῆς που ἄτερ λαῶν πόλιν ἐξέμεν Ε 472 f., and ἔχες δ' ἀλόχους κεδνὰς καὶ νήπια τέκνα
Ω 730 (Andromache is grieving for her dead husband), where
ἐξέμεν and ἔχες seem to be selected with reference to the
assumed etymology of Ἕκτωρ. Possibly there is a play on

the name of Odysseus in οὔ νύ τ᾽ Ὀδυσσεὺς .. τί νύ οἱ τόσον
ὠδύσαο Ζεῦ a 60 ff.; his name is explained (with doubtless
incorrect etymology) where his grandfather bestows it upon
him, ὀδυσσάμενος τόδ᾽ ἱκάνω .. τῷ δ᾽ Ὀδυσεὺς ὄνομ᾽ ἔστω ἐπώ-
νυμον τ 407 ff.; cf. ὀδύσαντο γὰρ αὐτῷ (Odysseus) | Ζεύς τε
καὶ Ἥέλιος τ 275 f., ὧδε Ποσειδάων ἐνοσίχθων | ὠδύσατ᾽ ἐκπά-
γλως ε 339 f.

d. The trick is well known which Odysseus played on
Polyphemus by assuming the name Οὖτις, ι 366, 408; cf.
the pun on μή τις and μῆτις, ι 410, 414: εἰ μὲν δὴ μή τίς σε
βιάζεται .. ἐμὸν δ᾽ ἐγέλασσε φίλον κῆρ | ὡς ὄνομ᾽ ἐξαπάτησεν
ἐμὸν καὶ μῆτις ἀμύμων. Another celebrated passage is concerning the ivory and horn gates of the dreams: οἱ μὲν [ὄνει-
ροι] κ᾽ ἔλθωσι διὰ πριστοῦ ἐλέφαντος, | οἵ ῥ᾽ ἐλεφαίρονται, ..
οἱ δὲ διὰ ξεστῶν κεράων ἔλθωσι θύραζε, | οἵ ῥ᾽ ἔτυμα κραίνουσι
τ 564 ff. But it is improbable that the similarity of sound is
intentional in ἕζετο (Helen) δ᾽ ἐν κλισμῷ, ὑπὸ δὲ θρῆνυς ποσὶν
(for the feet) ἦεν. | αὐτίκα δ᾽ ἥ γ᾽ ἐπέεσσι πόσιν (husband)
ἐρέεινεν ἕκαστα δ 136 f., or λέκτο (counted) δ᾽ ἀριθμόν .. ἔπειτα
δὲ λέκτο (lay down) καὶ αὐτός δ 451, 453.

e. COMPARISONS. A notable characteristic of Homeric
style is the comparison. This is designed to throw into high
relief some point in the action narrated; it often relieves
the monotony of the description of a battle. But the poet
is not always satisfied to illustrate the particular point for
which the comparison is introduced; he often completes the
picture by adding touches which have nothing to do with
the narrative, and is sometimes drawn on to add a new point
of comparison, as N 492 ff. There the Trojans are described
as following their leader, as sheep follow their bell-wether.
This scene is completed by adding to the original comparison the thought of the joy in the shepherd's heart as
he watches his orderly flock, and this suggests the second
comparison: "So Aeneas rejoiced at seeing the soldiers follow him."

f. Illustrations are furnished by all experiences of life, from
the lightning of Zeus and the conflict of opposing winds,
from the snow-storm and the mountain torrent, to a child
playing with the sand on the seashore, and a little girl cling-
ing to her mother's gown; from lions and eagles, to a stub-
born ass which refuses to be driven from a cornfield by children, and to a greedy fly; from the evening star to women
wrangling in the street. The lion is a special favorite, and
appears in comparisons thirty times in the Iliad. The Iliad
has but few illustrations drawn from the actions of men, such
as weaving (Ψ 760 ff.), tanning (P 389 ff.), or the grief of a
father for his dead son (Ψ 222 ff., *cf.* the delight of children
at their father's recovery from wasting disease, ε 394 ff.);
and but one from the operations of the mind (O 80 ff.),
where a traveler thinks of different places in rapid succession.

g. Homer, like Milton, could not think of an army in
motion without thinking of its resemblance to something
else. Just before the Catalogue of the Ships, the movements
of the Achaean armies are described by six detailed comparisons, B 455–483: the brightness of their armor is compared with the gleam of fire upon the mountains; their noisy
tumult, with the clamor of cranes or swans on the Asian
plain; in multitude, they are as the innumerable leaves and
flowers of spring-time; they are impetuous and bold as the
eager flies around the farm buildings; they are marshalled
by their leaders as flocks of goats by their herds; their
leader (Agamemnon) is like to Zeus, to Ares, to Poseidon,
— he is preëminent among the heroes as a bull in a herd of
cattle.

h. The Iliad has 182 detailed comparisons, 17 briefer (as
παισὶν ἐοικότες ἠγοράασθε | νηπιάχοις οἷς οὔ τι μέλει πολεμήια
ἔργα B 337 f.), and 28 of the briefest sort; the Odyssey has
39 detailed comparisons, 6 briefer, and 13 very brief. The
first book of the Iliad has only two comparisons, and those

of the briefest, ὁ δ' ἤιε νυκτὶ ἐοικώς Α 47, ἠΰτ' ὀμίχλη Α 359.
All the other books of the Iliad contain detailed comparisons; Π and Ρ have 20 each, Ν and Ο have 15 each, Λ has 14.

i. In comparisons, the poet sometimes makes reference to
customs that do not seem to have prevailed in the siege of
Troy: to riding on horseback (Ο 679), to the use of a kettle
for boiling meat (Φ 362), to the use of the trumpet in war
(Σ 219). This seems to imply a consciousness of change of
customs between heroic and Homeric times.

j. Comparisons are introduced by ὥς τε, ὡς εἰ, ὡς ὅτε, ὥς
περ κτλ.

Praepositive ὡς is not used in comparisons. In the briefest
comparisons, postpositive ὡς is often used, generally lengthening the preceding syllable (§§ 12 *l*, 41 *m*).

k. The aorist indicative (the so-called Gnomic aorist) is
often used in comparisons. The imperfect is found but
twice (Ο 274, Φ 495).

l. ASYNDETON. In the Homeric period more frequently
than in later Greek, sentences were left unconnected by
conjunctions, *i.e.* asyndeton (H. 1039) was allowed more
freely. It has been noticed above that ornamental epithets
are not connected by καί, and sometimes in animated discourse the poet uses no conjunction between clauses or
words, as ἀπριάτην ἀνάποινον Α 99.

m. Asyndeton of sentences is most frequent where the
second sentence explains the first and is in a kind of apposition with it, repeating the thought in a different form: ἀλλὰ
καὶ ὡς ἐθέλω δόμεναι πάλιν εἰ τό γ' ἄμεινον· | βούλομ' ἐγὼ
λαὸν σόον ἔμμεναι ἢ ἀπολέσθαι Α 116 f., ὦ πόποι, ἦ μέγα πέν-
θος 'Αχαιΐδα γαῖαν ἱκάνει· | ἦ κεν γηθήσαι Πρίαμος Πριάμοιό
τε παῖδες Α 254 f., ἀλλ' ὅδ' ἀνὴρ ἐθέλει περὶ πάντων ἔμμεναι
ἄλλων, | πάντων μὲν κρατέειν ἐθέλει πάντεσσι δ' ἀνάσσειν
Α 287 f. In Β 299, τλῆτε φίλοι καὶ μείνατ' ἐπὶ χρόνον gives
the sum of the preceding sentence, and the asyndeton marks
the speaker's warmth of feeling. Thus the second sentence

may express the result of the former, as ξεῖνε κακῶς ἀνδρῶν
τοξάζεαι · (therefore) οὐκέτ᾽ ἀέθλων | ἄλλων ἀντιάσεις χ 27 f.
An adversative relation is occasionally expressed by asynde-
ton, especially with γε μέν in the second clause, as Β 703,
Ε 516, Ω 642.

n. The absence of a conjunction often gives rapidity to
the style and thus is found often where the second sentence
begins with αὐτίκα or αἶψα, as εἰ δ᾽ ἄγε μὴν πείρησαι .. αἶψά
τοι αἷμα κελαινὸν ἐρωήσει περὶ δουρί Α 302 f., αὐτίκα κερτο-
μίοισι Δία Κρονίωνα προσηύδα Α 539, cf. Β 442. For the
tone of rapidity thus given to a narration, cf. δούπησεν δὲ
πεσών, ἀράβησε δὲ τεύχε᾽ ἐπ᾽ αὐτῷ · | αἵματί οἱ δεύοντο κόμαι
κτλ. Ρ 50 f.

Conjunctions are often omitted in excitement, as when
Achilles sees the flame flickering among the ships of the
Achaeans and calls to Patroclus ὄρσεο διογενὲς Πατρόκλεις
.. | λεύσσω δὴ παρὰ νηυσὶ πυρὸς δηίοιο ἰωήν · | μὴ δὴ νῆας
ἕλωσι .. | δύσεο τεύχεα θᾶσσον Π 126 ff.

o. CHIASMUS.[1] For emphasis, the poet sometimes so ar-
ranges the words of two clauses that the extremes, as also the
means, are correlative with or are contrasted with each other,
as παῖδά τε σοὶ ἀγέμεν, Φοίβῳ θ᾽ ἱερὴν ἑκατόμβην Α 443,
where παῖδα and ἑκατόμβην, σοί and Φοίβῳ respectively are
contrasted. Cf. ὡς Ἀχιλῆα | τιμήσῃς ὀλέσῃς δὲ πολέας Α
558 f., δυσμενέσιν μὲν χάρμα, κατηφείην δὲ σοὶ αὐτῷ Γ 51, ἄρν᾽,
ἕτερον λευκόν, ἑτέρην δὲ μέλαιναν, | Γῆ τε καὶ Ἡελίῳ Γ 103 f.,
where the black lamb was for Γῆ and the white for Ἡέλιος,
— βασιλεύς τ᾽ ἀγαθὸς κρατερός τ᾽ αἰχμητής Γ 179, where the
adjectives are brought together ; αὐτόν τ᾽ ἰσχανάασκον ἐρητύ-

---

[1] The name is given from the Greek letter X, there being a crossing of
ideas as

βασιλεύς τ᾽ ἀγαθός
κρατερός τ᾽ αἰχμητής Γ 179.

It should be noticed that this chiastic arrangement is often the most simple
and natural, as in the first example above, where σοί at once suggests the
other person interested, Φοῖβος.

ὀντό τε λαόν Ο 723.   *Cf.* Milton's "Sweet is the breath of
morn, her rising sweet," *Par. Lost* IV 641, " Adam the good-
liest man of men since born His 'sons, the fairest of her
daughters Eve," *Par. Lost* IV 323 f.

p. Epanalepsis.   Sometimes a word (generally a proper
name) or a clause is repeated in the same sentence at the
beginning of a new verse, as ἀλλ' ὁ μὲν Αἰθίοπας μετεκίαθε
τηλόθ' ἐόντας, | Αἰθίοπας τοὶ διχθὰ δεδαίαται κτλ. α 22 f. (the
only example in the Odyssey); τῷ δ' ἐγὼ ἀντίος εἶμι καὶ εἰ
πυρὶ χεῖρας ἔοικεν, | εἰ πυρὶ χεῖρας ἔοικε, μένος δ' αἴθωνι σιδήρῳ
Υ 371 f. *but I will go to meet him even if his hands are like to
fire, if his hands are like to fire and his might is like to bright
iron;* οὐ μέν πως νῦν ἔστιν .. | τῷ ὀαριζέμεναι ἅ τε παρθένος
ἠίθεός τε, | παρθένος ἠίθεός τ' ὀαρίζετον ἀλλήλοιιν Χ 126 ff.
*it is in no way possible now to chat with him as a maiden and
a young man, a maiden and a young man chat together.*   *Cf.*
Milton's *Lycidas* 37 f. "But O the heavy change, now thou
art gone, Now thou art gone and never must return."   The
name is repeated at the beginning of three successive verses
(Νιρεύς .. Νιρεύς .. Νιρεύς) Β 671 ff.   *Cf.* also Β 838, 850,
871, Ζ 154, Η 138, Μ 96, Φ 86, 158, Ψ 642.   The name when
repeated is attracted into the case of the following relative
pronoun in Ἀνδρομάχη, θυγάτηρ μεγαλήτορος Ἠετίωνος, | Ἠε-
τίων ὃς ἔναιεν ὑπὸ Πλάκῳ ὑληέσσῃ Ζ 395 f. *Andromache
daughter of the great-souled Eetion, Eetion who dwelt at the
foot of woody Placus.*

q. Similar to epanalepsis is the so-called ἐπιπλοκή, where
the finite verb is repeated in a participle, as μείδησεν δὲ βοῶ-
πις πότνια Ἥρη, | μειδήσασα δ' ἔπειτα ἑῷ ἐγκάτθετο κόλπῳ Ξ
222 f.; Τεῦκρος δ' ὡρμήθη μεμαὼς ἀπὸ τεύχεα δῦσαι, | Ἕκτωρ
δ' ὁρμηθέντος ἀκόντισε δουρὶ φαεινῷ Ν 182 f. *Teucer rushed,
eager to strip off his armor, but at him as he rushed, Hector
hurled his shining spear;* Ἕκτωρ ὡρμήθη .. | Αἴας δ' ὁρμηθέν-
τος ὀρέξατο Ἕκτορος Ν 188 ff.

r. Litotes (λιτότης or μείωσις), a *simplicity* of language,

or *understatement of the truth*, is common to all languages;
Milton's "unblest feet" is stronger than *cursed feet*. Homeric examples abound, as οὐκ Ἀγαμέμνονι ἥνδανε θυμῷ Α
24 *it was not pleasing to the soul of Agamemnon, i.e. it was
hateful, etc.;* ἂψ δ' ἐς κουλεὸν ὦσε μέγα ξίφος οὐδ' ἀπίθησεν |
μύθῳ Ἀθηναίης Α 220 f. *back into the sheath he thrust his
great sword nor did he disobey the word of Athene, i.e. he
obeyed;* Ἕκτωρ δ' οὔ τι θεᾶς ἔπος ἠγνοίησεν Β 807; οὐ κακόν
ἐστιν | τειρομένοις ἑτάροισιν ἀμυνέμεν αἰπὺν ὄλεθρον Σ 128 f.,
i.e. it is a noble thing, etc.; οὔ μιν ἀφαυρότατος βάλ' Ἀχαιῶν
Ο 11.

s. PERIPHRASIS. Certain periphrases occur frequently,
as ἄξετε δὲ Πριάμοιο βίην Γ 105 *bring the might of Priam, i.e.
the mighty Priam;* μετέειφ' ἱερὴ ἲς Τηλεμάχοιο β 409 *the
strength of Telemachus, etc.;* Παφλαγόνων δ' ἡγεῖτο Πυλαι-
μένεος λάσιον κῆρ Β 851; ὡς ἔπεσ' Ἕκτορος ὦκα χαμαὶ μένος
Ξ 418; ἐλθὼν γάρ ῥ' ἐκάκωσε βίη Ἡρακληείη Λ 690, where the
gender of the participle shows that βίη Ἡρακληείη is equivalent to Ἡρακλέης, which (— — ◡ —) was not suited to dactylic
verse; τοίου γὰρ κλέος ἐσθλὸν ἀπώλεσαν ἡνιόχοιο Ψ 280, for
τοῖον εὐκλεία ἡνίοχον κτλ.; τὰ τείρεα πάντα . . τό τε σθένος
Ὠρίωνος Σ 485 f. *all the constellations . . the force of Orion;*
ἢ ἔπει ὤνησας κραδίην Διὸς ἠὲ καὶ ἔργῳ Α 395.

δούλιον ἦμαρ Ζ 463 is simply a poetic expression for *slav-
ery*, ἐλεύθερον ἦμαρ Τ 193 for *freedom*, ὀλέθριον ἦμαρ Τ 294
for *destruction*, ἦμαρ ὀρφανικόν Χ 490 for *the state of orphan-
age*, νόστιμον ἦμαρ α 9 for *return*.

t. ZEUGMA. Sometimes two connected subjects or objects
are made to depend on a verb which is appropriate to but
one of them, as ἢ μὲν ἔπειτα | εἰς ἅλα ἆλτο . . | Ζεὺς δὲ ἑὸν
πρὸς δῶμα (*sc.* ἔβη) Α 531 ff. *she then leaped into the sea, but
Zeus went to his own house;* ἧχι ἑκάστου | ἵπποι ἀερσίποδες
καὶ ποικίλα τεύχε' ἔκειτο Γ 326 f. *where the high-stepping
horses of each were standing and the bright armor was
lying;* ἔδουσί τε πίονα μῆλα | οἶνόν τ' ἔξαιτον μελιηδέα Μ

319 f.; Κυκλώπων δ' ἐς γαῖαν ἐλεύσσομεν ἐγγὺς ἐόντων, | καπ-
νόν τ' αὐτῶν τε φθογγὴν οἴων τε καὶ αἰγῶν ι 166 f.; ἔσσατο δ'
ἔκτοσθεν ῥινὸν πολιοῖο λύκοιο, | κρατὶ δ' ἐπὶ κτιδέην κυνέην
Κ 334 f. *Cf*. Shakespeare, *Sonnet* 55, 7 "Nor Mars his sword,
nor war's quick fire shall burn | The living record of your
memory."

u. Hysteron Proteron. Occasionally the more important or obvious object or action is mentioned before another
which should precede it in strict order of time, as ἅμα τράφεν
ἠδὲ γένοντο Α 251 *were bred and born with him* (*cf*. Shake-
speare *Twelfth Night* I ii "For I was bred and born | Not
three hours' travel from this very place."), γαμέοντί τε γει-
νομένῳ τε δ 208 *to him as he is married and born*, εἵματά τ'
ἀμφιέσασα θυώδεα καὶ λούσασα ε 264 *putting about him per-
fumed garments and bathing him*, χλαῖνάν τε χιτῶνά τε ἕννυτ'
Ὀδυσσεύς ε 229 *Odysseus put about him cloak and tunic*, αὐ-
τούς τ' ἀμβαίνειν ἀνά τε πρυμνήσια λῦσαι ι 178 *both themselves
to embark and to loose the stern hawsers*, οἳ δ' ἄνεσάν τε πύλας
καὶ ἀπῶσαν ὀχῆας Φ 537.

v. Later Change in Words. The student must be
watchful to apprehend the exact Homeric meaning of words
which are used in a slightly different sense in later Greek.
Thus ἀγορή and ἀγών are used in Homer of an *assembly*,
gathering, not of *market* and *contest*. Ἀΐδης is always the
name of a person, not of a place. ἀοιδός, ἀοιδή, are used
for the Attic ποιητής, ὕμνος, — ἔπος is used for λόγος (only
Ο 393, *a* 56), θεσμός for νομος, κοσμέω for τάσσω. δεινός
means *terrible*, not *skillful*. δεῖπνον is the principal meal of
the day, whenever it is taken. ἔγχος means *spear*, never
sword. ἥρως is used of all the warriors; it does not mean
a *hero* in the English sense. θύω is used not of sacrifices in
general, but of the burning of the ἀπαρχαί ("first fruits")
or θυηλαί to the gods. θαυμάζω often means only *watch in-
tently*. κρίνω is *select, discriminate*, rather than *judge*. νοέω
often has the sense of αἰσθάνομαι (which is not Homeric),

perceive. ὄνομαι is not *blame* in a general way, but *think
not enough, insufficient.* οὐτάζω is *wound with a weapon held
in the hand,* not with a missile. πέμπω is *escort, attend,* as
well as *send ;* cf. πομπή *convoy,* πομπός *a guide,* and πομπή,
in Attic, *procession.* πόλεμος is often *battle* rather than *war.*
πρήσσω is *carry through* rather than *do* as in Attic. σχεδόν
is *near,* of place, not *almost.* σῶμα is used only of a *dead
body,* δέμας being used of the living form, and αὐτός and
περὶ χροΐ taking some of the Attic uses of σῶμα. τάχα
always means *quickly,* never *perhaps* as in later Greek.
τίθημι is often used like ποιέω *make.* φόβος is not *fright*
but *flight ;* φοβέομαι is not *fear* but *flee ;* φύζα is *flight* with
the added notion of fear or shame. φράζω is *point out,* not
say. ὡς does not mean *since.*

w. The accent of some words is not the same as in Attic,
as ἴδε P 179 for the Attic ἰδέ; in ἶσος (Attic ἴσος) and φᾶρος
(Attic φάρος), this results from the difference in quantity
(§ 41 *f* γ). The ancient grammarians call ἑτοῖμος, ἐρῆμος,
ὁμοῖος, γελοῖος ὄργυια the Homeric and older forms for ἕτοι-
μος, ἔρημος, κτλ., and ὀργυιά. Cf. μυρία *countless number,* for
the Attic μύρια *ten thousand.*

x. αἰθήρ is feminine in Homer, as Π 365; masculine in
Attic. κίων is sometimes feminine, as *a* 127; sometimes
masculine, as θ 66. Ἴλιος is feminine in Homer (except perhaps O 71), but neuter (Ἴλιον) in prose.

y. The absence from the Homeric vocabulary of αἰσθάνομαι, λόγος, ποιητής, τάσσω, ὕμνος has been noted above. To
this list may be added ἀνδράποδα (only H 475), ἄρτος (only
ρ 343, σ 120, elsewhere σῖτος is used instead), βάρβαρος (but
βαρβαρόφωνος B 867), δεῖ (only I 337), δοῦλος (but δούλη
Γ 409, δ 12, δουλοσύνη χ 423, δούλιον ἦμαρ thrice, δούλειον
ω 252), ἐπιχειρῶ, ἑσπέρα (but ἕσπερος and ἑσπέριος), ζητῶ,
κυνηγέτης (only ι 120, elsewhere θηρητήρ), μέρος (μοῖρα takes
its place), μεταξύ (only A 156, elsewhere μεσσηγύς), μίασμα,
μισέω (only P 272), πενίη (only ξ 157, πενιχρός γ 348), πορεύ-

ομαι, σοφός, σοφίη (only O 412), σπείρω (but σπέρμα once,
ε 490), τάξις.

HOMERIC SYNTAX.

§ 3. a. In syntax as in forms, where the Homeric dialect
differs from the Attic, it may be presumed that the Homeric
usage is the earlier. The language was less rigid; custom
had not yet established certain constructions as normal.
There was greater freedom in the use of the modes and the
cases, of prepositions and conjunctions.

b. It is impossible to bring the Homeric uses of the modes
under the categories and rules that prevailed in the Attic
period. Intermediate in force between the simple future and
the potential optative with ἄν were

(1) the subjunctive as a less vivid future, as οὐ γάρ πω
τοίους ἴδον ἀνέρας οὐδὲ ἴδωμαι A 262 *I never yet saw such men
nor shall I see them;*

(2) the subjunctive with κέν or ἄν, as a potential mode,
as εἰ δέ κε μὴ δώωσιν ἐγὼ δέ κεν αὐτὸς ἕλωμαι A 137 *but if
they shall not give it, I myself will then take, etc.;* τῶν κέν τις
τόδ' ἔχῃσιν ἐπεὶ θάνε δῖος Ὀδυσσεύς a 396 *of these some one
may have this honor since divine Odysseus perished;* οὐκ ἄν
τοι χραίσμῃ κίθαρις Γ 54 *the cithara would not in that case
avail thee;*

(3) the potential optative without ἄν, as ῥεῖα θεός γ' ἐθέ-
λων καὶ τηλόθεν ἄνδρα σαώσαι γ 231 *easily could a god if he
wished bring a man home in safety even from a distant land.*

Examples of the future indicative with ἄν are rare and
the correctness of the text is doubted. Thus κεν μελήσει
P 515 may have been an error of the scribe for κεν μελήσῃ in
transferring from the old alphabet (§ 4 *i*).

c. *a.* Homer prefers εἰ with the subjunctive to εἴ κεν (αἴ κεν) or εἰ ἄν with the subjunctive. εἰ ἄν is not used in general conditions.

β. εἴ κεν is rarely used with the optative (29 times in all); never in the expression of a wish. εἰ ἄν is used with the optative but once, εἴ περ ἂν αὐταὶ | μοῦσαι ἀείδοιεν B 597 f.

γ. εἰ with the optative to express indefinite frequency of past action, is found but once, ἀλλ᾽ εἴ τίς με καὶ ἄλλος ἐνὶ μεγάροισιν ἐνίπτοι Ω 768 *but if (whenever) even another in the palace upbraided me.*

δ. The optative in indirect discourse is used for the indicative in direct discourse only in questions, except εἰπεῖν, ὡς ἔλθοι καὶ ἴκοιτ᾽ ἐς πατρίδα γαῖαν ω 237.

ε. In six passages the optative with κέν is used in the apodosis, where Homeric and Attic usage alike lead us to expect ἄν with a past tense of the indicative, as καί νύ κεν ἔνθ᾽ ἀπόλοιτο ἄναξ ἀνδρῶν Αἰνείας, | εἰ μὴ ἄρ᾽ ὀξὺ νόησε Διὸς θυγάτηρ Ἀφροδίτη E 311 f. "Aeneas would have perished if Aphrodite had not perceived," *etc.*

ζ. κέν is used four times as frequently as ἄν. ἄν is more common in negative than in affirmative sentences.

d. The cases retained more of their original force than in Attic and had less need of a preposition to make the construction distinct (it was once thought that the poet omitted the preposition for the convenience of his verse), as the ablatival genitive in Τρῶας ἄμυνε νεῶν O 731 *he was warding off the Trojans from the ships,* ἕρκος Ἀχαιοῖσιν πέλεται πολέμοιο κακοῖο A 284 *is a bulwark for the Achaeans from* (to keep off) *evil war,* καρπαλίμως ἀνέδυ πολιῆς ἁλὸς ἠΰτ᾽ ὀμίχλη A 359 *swiftly she rose as a mist out of the hoary sea.* The dative of place is often found without a preposition, as τόξ᾽ ὤμοισιν ἔχων A 45 *having his bow upon his shoulder.*

The prepositions still retained much of their adverbial nature, and had not become fixedly attached to the verbs which they modified (§ 37). It was once thought that the

occasional separation of verb and preposition was a poetic
license, and (considered as a surgical operation) it was called
tmesis.

e. In the Homeric period certain constructions were only
beginning to appear definitely in use, as the accusative with
the infinitive and the genitive absolute. The infinitive was
assuming more and more the character of an indeclinable
noun, but is not found with the article. ὥστε with the infinitive of result is found but twice, and these passages are
thought to be corrupt; this construction is found but four
times in Pindar's odes.

f. *a.* The genitive absolute is more frequent with the
present participle (52 examples, 28 in Iliad and 24 in Odyssey, — not quite half being temporal) than with the aorist
participle (21 examples, 17 in Iliad and 4 in Odyssey, —
only 7 being strictly temporal). The genitive absolute with
omitted subject is particularly rare, and is denied by most
scholars; but an approach to it is made in expressions like
Τηλέμαχος δ᾿ ἐν μὲν κραδίῃ μέγα πένθος ἄεξεν | βλημένου
ρ 489 f., where the participle agrees with Ὀδυσῆος to be supplied, as genitive of cause. The participle sometimes seems
to be used with omitted subject when it really agrees with
the genitive implied in a preceding dative (*g.* γ below).

β. It is often impossible to say categorically whether the
genitive is in the absolute construction or rather depends on
some other word, as ὑπὸ δὲ Τρῶες κεχάδοντο | ἀνδρὸς ἀκοντίσ-
σαντος Δ 497 f., where the position of the genitive at the beginning of the verse gives it greater independence, but it was
probably influenced by the verb: *the Trojans drew back from
the man as he hurled his javelin;* cf. ἔκλαγξαν δ᾿ ἄρ᾿ ὀιστοὶ
ἐπ᾿ ὤμων χωομένοιο | αὐτοῦ κινηθέντος Α 46 f.

γ. Sometimes a preposition is used where the genitive
absolute would be used in Attic prose, as ἀμφὶ δὲ νῆες | σμερ-
δαλέον κονάβησαν ἀυσάντων ὑπ᾿ Ἀχαιῶν Β 333 f.

g. *a.* The dative of interest is often used with the verb

where the English idiom prefers a possessive genitive with a
noun, as δεινὼ δέ οἱ ὄσσε φάανθεν Α 200 *terribly did her* (lit.
for her the) *eyes gleam;* θεὰ δέ οἱ ἔκλυεν ἀρῆς δ 767 *the goddess heard her prayer* (lit. *for her the prayer*); or is used
instead of an ablatival genitive with a preposition, as Δαναοῖ-
σιν ἀεικέα λοιγὸν ἀπώσει Α 97 *will ward off ignominious destruction from* (lit. *for*) *the Danaï;* or instead of a genitive
with verbs of ruling and leading, as πάντεσσι δ᾽ ἀνάσσειν
Α 288 *to reign over* (lit. *be the king for*) *all;* (Ζεὺς) ὃς πᾶσι
θνητοῖσι καὶ ἀθανάτοισιν ἀνάσσει Μ 242; or instead of the
dative with a preposition, as τοῖσι δ᾽ ἀνέστη Α 68 *for them
rose* (not to be taken as a local dative, *among them*), while
in ἐν Ἀργείοισιν ἀναστάς Τ 175 the poet presents the same
general idea from another point of view.

β. This dative of interest is used even of things, as κελσά-
σῃσι δὲ νηυσὶ καθείλομεν ἱστία πάντα ι 149 *when the ships
were beached* (lit. *for the ships when they were beached*) *we
lowered all the sails.*

γ. This dative was felt to be equivalent to the genitive,
and is often followed by a participle or adjective in the geni-
tive, as ἡμῖν δ᾽ αὖτε κατεκλάσθη φίλον ἦτορ | δεισάντων φθόγ-
γον τε βαρὺν αὐτόν τε πέλωρον ι 256 f. *our dear hearts sank
within us, as fear came upon us,* etc., where δεισάντων agrees
with the ἡμῶν implied in ἡμῖν.

h. a. The dative is used with σύν or ἄμα, corresponding
to μετά with the genitive in Attic prose; in this sense even
μετά is occasionally used with the dative (almost always
plural), as ἐπέτοντο μετὰ πνοίης ἀνέμοιο β 148 *they flew (i.e.
kept pace) with the blasts of the wind;* cf. ἄμα πνοιῆς ἀνέμοιο
a 98, the simple dative of association πέτετο πνοιῆς ἀνέμοιο
Μ 207.

β. ἐπί is used with the dative in the same sense of hostility
as with the accusative in Attic, as ὦρσεν ἐπ᾽ Ἀργείοισι Μ 293
roused him against the Argives; cf. ἔπεσθαι ἐπὶ βασιλέα Xen.
An. I 4. 14.

γ. ὑπό is used with the dative in almost the same sense
as with the genitive in Attic, as ἐδάμη ὑπὸ χερσὶ ποδώκεος
Αἰακίδαο Β 860 *he was slain by the hands of the swift-footed
Aeacides*, with perhaps more of the original local force of the
preposition.

i. Some constructions were used more freely and constantly than in later Greek. Certain of these were always
looked upon as poetic, as θείη πεδίοιο Ζ 507 *shall run over
the plain;* ἐπέτοντο κονίοντες πεδίοιο θ 122 *flew hastening (cov-
ered with dust) over the plain* (genitive of the place to which
the action belongs, H. 760; G. 179, 2); πυρὸς θερέω ρ 23
warm at the fire; μνηστῆρας ἀφίκετο α 332 *she came to the
suitors.*

j. A neuter noun in the plural is the subject of a plural
verb more frequently than in Attic. The imperfect is more
freely used in narrative, to describe an action as in progress.
The historical present is not used. ἐστί is not always a
mere copula, and is occasionally modified by an adverb as
a true verb of existence, *cf.* ἐπεί νύ τοι αἶσα μίνυνθά περ, οὔ
τι μάλα δήν Α 416 *since thy appointed time of life is brief, etc.*,
with μίνυνθα | ἡμέων ἔσσεται ἦδος Λ 317 f. *brief shall be the
good from us*, and μίνυνθα δέ οἱ γένεθ᾽ ὁρμή Δ 466 *but brief
was his onset.*

k. χρή is still a noun, construed like χρειώ, χρεώ with a
genitive of the thing needed and occasionally an accusative
of the person (the accusative of limit of motion with some
verb like ἱκάνεται or γίγνεται supplied in thought); *cf.* τέο
σε χρή δ 463 *of what hast thou need*, with τίνα χρειὼ τόσον
ἵκει β 28 and ἐμὲ δὲ χρεὼ γίγνεται αὐτῆς δ 634.

χρῆναι, χρέων, ἐχρῆν, χρῆν κτλ. are not Homeric; δεῖ is
found only Ι 337. While verbals in -τος are more freely employed than in Attic, verbals in -τέος are not used.

l. *a.* PARTICLES. The beginner in reading Homer is per-
plexed by a large number of particles that are often difficult
to render by English words. Their force can often be best

given by the order of the words in the translation or by the
tone of voice in reading; to translate ῥά *as was natural* (or
even *you see*) or γέ *at least*, often throws upon the particle
very disproportionate emphasis. The student can most easily
and clearly appreciate the force of a particle by comparing a
number of examples which have become familiar to him; he
will then see the importance of these particles to the character and tone of a speech or of the narrative.

β. It is to be noted that in Homer δή may stand at the beginning of a clause. τέ is used far more freely than in Attic
prose; a single τέ often being used to connect single notions,
as κύνεσσιν | οἰωνοῖσί τε A 4 f. The poet does not use οὔκουν,
καίτοι, τοίνυν, δῆτα, δῆθεν, εἶτα (but ἔπειτα), or the causal
ἅτε. ὥς, δή, and γέ are less frequent than in Attic.

γ. ὅπως is rare as a final particle, occurring only about a
dozen times; ὄφρα is the usual particle to introduce a final
clause.

m. a. INTERROGATIVE PARTICLES. The general interrogative particle in Homer is ἦ, but in a double question (where
the Attic Greek uses πότερον . . ἤ) ἤ or ἠέ stands in the first
member, ἦ or ἦε in the second, as τοῦτ᾽ ἀγόρευσον . . | ἠὲ νέον
μεθέπεις, ἦ καὶ πατρώιός ἐσσι | ξεῖνος a 174 ff. *tell me this . .
whether thou art come for the first time or whether thou hast
been a guest of my father;* cf. A 190 ff., Γ 239 f. Where the
questions are less closely connected, ἦ may introduce each,
as ὦ ξεῖνοι, τίνες ἐστέ; πόθεν πλεῖθ᾽ ὑγρὰ κέλευθα; | ἦ τι κατὰ
πρῆξιν; ἦ μαψιδίως ἀλάλησθε | οἷά τε ληιστῆρες γ 71 ff.
*Strangers, who are ye?　Whence sail ye the watery ways?
Sail ye on trade?　Or are ye wandering idly like pirates?*

β. When ἦ introduces a single question, it is rarely used
as in Attic, as a mere interrogation point; it regularly implies emotion of some kind. This ἦ διαπορητικός (of interrogation) is still closely allied with the ἦ βεβαιωτικός (of
asseveration), but the ἦ διαπορητικός must be carefully dis-
tinguished from the ἦ διαζευκτικός (*disjunctive*).

γ. The interrogative ἆρα is not Homeric.

n. PARATAXIS. The Homeric language is far less distinct than the Latin or the English in the expression of logical relations, and gives less prominence to the logical forms of syntax; but it is seldom difficult to appreciate the ancient idiom if an attempt is made to find the Homeric point of view.

The Homeric poems contain many survivals of the simplest form of sentences. In the earliest stage of the Greek language clauses were not combined with each other as secondary and principal; they were simply added one to the other. To use the technical terms, *coördination* or *parataxis* (παράταξις) was the rule, — not *subordination* or *hypotaxis* (ὑπόταξις). Hypotaxis was not possible until the language had relative pronouns or subordinate conjunctions to serve as joints to connect the clauses; but originally the relatives were demonstratives, and relative sentences have been called parenthetic demonstrative sentences. Thus δέ was used in the apodosis of relative and conditional sentences; this was especially frequent when the relative or conditional clause preceded, as εἰ δέ κε μὴ δώωσιν, ἐγὼ δέ κεν αὐτὸς ἕλωμαι Α 137 *but if they shall not give it, (but) I myself shall then take,* etc.; εἶος ὁ ταῦθ' ὥρμαινε . . ἦλθε δ' Ἀθήνη Α 193 f. *while he was pondering this* . . *(but) Athena came;* οἵη περ φύλλων γενεή, τοίη δὲ καὶ ἀνδρῶν Ζ 146 *as is the race of leaves, (but) such is also the race of men.* So αὐτάρ and ἀλλά are used with stronger emphasis than δέ, as εἰ δὲ σὺ καρτερός ἐσσι, θεὰ δέ σε γείνατο μήτηρ | ἀλλ' ὅδε φέρτερός ἐστιν ἐπεὶ πλεόνεσσιν ἀνάσσει Α 280 f. *but if thou art mighty and a goddess is thy mother, but,* etc., where the apodosis is really contrasted with the protasis, *cf.* Α 81 quoted in the next paragraph.

o. Compare with the foregoing the use of καί in the conclusion of relative sentences, to mark the connection of the clauses, as ἀλλ' ὅτε τέτρατον ἦλθεν ἔτος . . | καὶ τότε δή τις ἔειπε β 107 f. *but when the fourth year came (and) then some*

one told etc.; ἦμος δ' ἠριγένεια φάνη ῥοδοδάκτυλος Ἠώς, | καὶ
τότ' ἐγὼν ἀγορὴν θέμενος κτλ. ι 170 f. *but when Dawn appeared*
.. (*and*) *then I called together etc.*   Thus also τέ was freely
used in subordinate clauses, as ὅς κε θεοῖς ἐπιπείθηται μάλα τ'
ἔκλυον αὐτοῦ Α 218 *whoever obeys the gods,* (*and*) *himself the
gods readily hear;* and τέ — τέ is found in both protasis and
apodosis, marking their correlation, as εἴ περ γάρ τε χόλον ..
καταπέψῃ, | ἀλλά τε καὶ μετόπισθεν ἔχει κότον Α 81 f. *for
even if he should restrain his wrath, but even hereafter etc.*

p. The first part of a paratactic sentence may introduce the
cause or reason for what follows, as in Andromache's words
to Hector, Ἕκτορ ἀτὰρ σύ μοί ἐσσι πατὴρ καὶ πότνια μήτηρ, |
ἠδὲ κασίγνητος, σὺ δέ μοι θαλερὸς παρακοίτης · | ἀλλ' ἄγε νῦν
ἐλέαιρε καὶ αὐτοῦ μίμν' ἐπὶ πύργῳ Ζ 429 ff. *But thou, Hector,
art my father etc.*, which implies "Hector, since thou art
my all."

q. CORRELATIVE CONSTRUCTIONS.   The Greek language
was always fond of a parallel or antithetic construction, a
contrast, a balance, where the English subordinates one
thought to the other; but the adversative relation, where
the English idiom would use a subordinate clause introduced
by *for, although, when, while,* or *since,* is more frequent in
these poems than in later Greek, as ὅς οἱ πλησίον ἷζε μάλιστα
δέ μιν φιλέεσκεν η 171 *who sat near him for* (lit. *but*) *he was
his favorite;* ἀλλὰ πίθεσθ' · ἄμφω δὲ νεωτέρω ἐστὸν ἐμεῖο Α
259; ῥεῖά τ' ἀριγνώτη πέλεται, καλαὶ δέ τε πᾶσαι ζ 108 *she is
easily recognized although* (lit. *but*) *all are beautiful;* Ἠὼς δὲ
κροκόπεπλος ἐκίδνατο πᾶσαν ἐπ' αἶαν | οἳ δ' εἰς ἄστυ ἕλων
Ω 695 f. *Dawn was spreading her rays over the whole earth
when* (lit. *but*) *these drove into the city; (cf.* δύσετό τ' ἠέλιος
καὶ τοὶ κλυτὸν ἄλσος ἵκοντο ζ 321 *the sun set and these came
etc.*, for *as the sun set etc.*, a construction which is not rare
in English or in later Greek, as καὶ ἤδη τε ἦν περὶ πλή-
θουσαν ἀγορὰν καὶ ἔρχονται παρὰ βασιλέως καὶ Τισσαφέρνους
κήρυκες Xen. *An.* II i. 7 "when it was about the time ..

heralds come" *etc.*) ; φύλλα τὰ μέν τ' ἄνεμος χαμάδις χέει,
ἀλλὰ δέ θ' ὕλη | τηλεθόωσα φύει, ἔαρος δ' ἐπιγίγνεται ὥρη
Z 147 f. . . *when the season of Spring comes on;* ἢ οὐχ ἅλις
ὡς τὸ πάροιθεν ἐκείρετε πολλὰ καὶ ἐσθλὰ | κτήματ' ἐμά, μνη-
στῆρες, ἐγὼ δ' ἔτι νήπιος ἦα β 312 f., where the last clause is
equivalent to ἐμοῦ ἔτι νηπίου ὄντος, — ἠμὲν δή ποτ' ἐμεῦ πάρος
ἔκλυες εὐξαμένοιο . . ἠδ' ἔτι καὶ νῦν μοι τόδ' ἐπικρήηνον ἐέλδωρ
A 453 ff. *as thou didst hear my former prayer so now also
fulfil this my desire;* κρείσσων μὲν Ζεὺς . . κρείσσων αὖτε Διὸς
γενεὴ κτλ. Φ 190 f. *as Zeus is mightier than the rivers, so is
the race of Zeus etc.*

r. αὐτάρ also is used where a causal particle would be used
in English, as ὀδύνῃσι πεπαρμένος · αὐτὰρ οἰστὸς | ὤμῳ ἐνὶ
στιβαρῷ ἠλήλατο E 399 f. *thrilled with pains since the arrow
was fixed in his stout shoulder.*

In these contrasted clauses, αὖ, αὖτε, αὐτάρ, ἀτάρ, ἀλλά, as
well as δέ, may be used in correlation with μέν.

s. A copulative conjunction is sometimes used where the
English uses a disjunctive *or*, as τριπλῇ τετραπλῇ τε A 128
threefold or (and) fourfold, in which prominence is given to
the second member, as in δεκάκις τε καὶ εἰκοσάκις I 379 ; *cf.*
ἕνα καὶ δύο B 346, χθιζά τε καὶ πρωιζά B 303, τριχθά τε καὶ
τετραχθά Γ 363, πεντάετές γε καὶ ἑξάετες γ 115, τρὶς μάκαρες
καὶ τετράκις ε 306 (*O terque quaterque beati,* Verg. *Aen.* I 94).
Cf. εὖ τε καὶ χεῖρον Thuc. II 35 *better or worse, bis terque*
Hor. *A. P.* 440, *rarus duabus tribusque civitatibus conventus*
Tac. *Agric.* 12.

t. The Homeric poet sometimes puts into an independent
clause the incidental thought which in later Greek would be
expressed regularly by a participle, as λαοὶ δ' ἠρήσαντο θεοῖς
ἰδὲ χεῖρας ἀνέσχον Γ 318 *the people prayed to the gods with
uplifted hands* (lit. *and lifted their hands*) for χεῖρας ἀνα-
σχόντες, *cf.* μεγάλ' εὔχετο, χεῖρας ἀνασχών A 450 ; (Ζεὺς μερ-
μήριζε ὡς Ἀχιλῆα) τιμήσῃ, ὀλέσῃ δὲ πολέας ἐπὶ νηυσὶν Ἀχαιῶν
B 4 *was pondering how he might honor Achilles by destroying*

(lit. *and destroy*) etc.; βῆ ῥ᾽ ἴμεν εἰς ἀγορήν, παλάμῃ δ᾽ ἔχε χάλκεον ἔγχος β 10 for βῆ ἔχων κτλ., *cf.* ἦλθε φέρων, ἔχων Α 12 f.; ἀλλ᾽ ἀκέουσα κάθησο, ἐμῷ δ᾽ ἐπιπείθεο μύθῳ Α 565 for ἐμῷ πειθομένη μύθῳ, — τόνδε λίσσοντο γέροντες | Αἰτωλῶν πέμπον δὲ θεῶν ἱερῆας Ι 575 "they sent the priests of the gods to supplicate him"; οὐδ᾽ ἔλαθ᾽ Αἴαντα . . | Ζεύς, ὅτε δὴ Τρώ-εσσι δίδου ἑτεραλκέα νίκην Ρ 626 f. for οὐδ᾽ ἔλαθε διδοὺς κτλ. See § 1 *e*.

u. This use is sometimes striking in comparisons, as ὥς τε σφῆκες . . οἰκία ποιήσωνται ὁδῷ ἔπι παιπαλοέσσῃ, | οὐδ᾽ ἀπο-λείπουσιν . . ἀλλὰ μένοντες . . ἀμύνονται περὶ τέκνων Μ 167 ff. *as wasps build their houses near a rocky road, nor do they abandon them, but remain and defend their children*, where the point of comparison lies not at all in οἴκια ποιήσωνται κτλ. but wholly in the οὐδ᾽ ἀπολείπουσιν κτλ. See § 2 *e*.

v. Conversely, the participle, as in later Greek, often con-tains the principal idea, as μυρομένοισι δὲ τοῖσι φάνη ῥοδοδά-κτυλος Ἠώς Ψ 109 "they wept until Dawn appeared"; τοῖσι δὲ τερπομένοισι μέλας ἐπὶ ἕσπερος ἦλθεν α 423; ὄφρα λείψαντε κιοίτην Ω 285; κατένευσεν | Ἴλιον ἐκπέρσαντ᾽ εὐτείχεον ἀπο-νέεσθαι Β 113 *promised that I should sack Ilios and return;* but in the very next verse is the English idiom, νῦν δὲ κακὴν ἀπάτην βουλεύσατο, καί με κελεύει | δυσκλέα Ἄργος ἱκέσθαι Β 114 f. *planned an evil deceit and bids me go* etc., for ἀπά-την βουλεύσας. The two constructions are interchanged in ἐτύχησε βαλών Ο 581 and τυχήσας βεβλήκει Δ 106 ff.

THE HOMERIC DIALECT.

§ 4. a. The dialect of the Homeric poems is in one sense artificial: it was spoken at no place and at no time. But it is not a mosaic composed of words and forms chosen capri-ciously from the different Greek dialects; it is a product of

natural growth.   It was developed under the influence of
the dactylic hexameter by successive generations of bards
who preserved obsolete or obsolescent words, phrases, and
forms which were suited to their verse, and who adopted also
from the common speech of their own times what was avail-
able for their use.   Thus older and newer forms subsisted
side by side, just as the English poet can choose between
loveth and *loves, lovéd* and *lov'd, aye* and *éver.*   The poets
unconsciously excluded all that was not adapted to dactylic
verse, but they did no violence to their language ; they did
not wantonly change quantities or introduce new terminations.   " The dialect did not spring from a formless linguistic
dough kneaded in the trough of the verse."

b.   This conservation of old forms together with the introduction of new forms was very convenient for the verse;
e.g. for the infinitive of the verb *be,* Homer could use ἔμμεναι as dactyl, _ ◡ ◡ ; ἔμεναι as anapaest, ◡ ◡ _ ; ἔμμεν as
trochee, _ ◡ ; ἔμεν as pyrrhic, ◡ ◡ ; εἶναι as spondee, _ _ .
Naturally, the choice being offered, metrical convenience determined which of these forms should be used.   Metrical
convenience often or generally decided between the use of
Ἀχαιοί or Ἀργεῖοι.

c.   The same is true in the case of synonyms and stock epithets or phrases ; Homer uses δῖος as a disyllable, θεῖος (better
written θέιος) where he wishes a trisyllable, as δῖος Ὀδυσσεύς,
but Ὀδυσσῆος θείοιο at the close of a verse.   The most frequently recurring epithets of Odysseus are πολύτλας, πολύμητις, πολυμήχανος, ταλασίφρων, ποικιλομήτης, — all of different metrical value.   ἄναξ ἀνδρῶν Ἀγαμέμνων is used after
the feminine caesura (§ 40 *f*) of the third foot, but εὐρὺ κρείων
Ἀγαμέμνων, Ἀγαμέμνονος Ἀτρείδαο, or Ἀγαμέμνονα ποιμένα
λαῶν after the masculine caesura of the same foot.   Πηληιάδεω
Ἀχιλῆος is used after the penthemimeral caesura (§ 40 *e*), πόδας ὠκὺς Ἀχιλλεύς after the hephthemimeral caesura (§ 40 *g*),
but ποδάρκης δῖος Ἀχιλλεύς, ποδώκεος Αἰακίδαο or ἀμύμονος

Αἰακίδαο, ποδάρκεϊ Πηλεΐωνι, ποδώκεα Πηλείωνα, ἀμύμονα Πηλείωνα, or Ἀχιλλῆα πτολίπορθον, after the feminine caesura
of the third foot, with δῖος Ἀχιλλεύς as a tag when the verse
is filled up to the Bucolic diaeresis (§ 40 *h*). *Cf.* the epithets
of Apollo, ἑκάτοιο A 385 ∪∪‒∪, ἑκηβόλου A 14 ∪‒∪∪,
ἑκάεργος A 479 ∪∪‒∪, ἑκατηβόλου A 370 ∪∪‒∪∪, ἑκατη-
βελέταο A 75 ∪∪‒∪∪‒∪. See § 1 *q*.

d. The convenience of the verse decided whether the poet
should say ὡς φάτο (before a consonant) or ὡς ἔφατ᾽ (before
a vowel), ἑταῖρος or ἔταρος (§ 5 *h*), πάννυχος or παννύχιος,
μόριμος or μόρσιμος, κεῖνος or ἐκεῖνος. αἶα is used as well as
γαῖα, but only at the close of the verse, where other old forms
are preserved, as ἀπὸ πατρίδος αἴης a 75; *cf.* ἐς πατρίδα γαῖαν
B 174; while γῆ is used half a dozen times, as Γ 104. In
this way the Homeric poems doubtless had considerable influence on the language, assisting in the preservation of old
words and forms and in the establishment in use of new
words and forms which were metrically convenient.

e. The dialect is essentially Ionic and seems to have origi-
nated among the Ionians of Asia Minor, influenced possibly
by the speech and certainly far more by the old poems of
their Aeolian neighbors. The oldest form of Greek Epic
songs seems to have been Aeolic, but the Ionians brought
Epic poetry to perfection. Even the Pythian priestess de-
livered the oracles of Apollo in Epic verse and Ionic dialect,
and the Dorian Spartans sang about their camp-fires the
Ionian songs of Tyrtaeus. Homer, however, does not have
certain marked Ionic peculiarities, as κῶς, κότε for πῶς, πότε.

f. A considerable number of Aeolisms is found in the
poems, especially in certain phrases and in certain feet of
the verse, as ἄλλυδις ἄλλος, ὕπαιθα. This traditional Aeolic
influence appears still more marked in the survival of the
digamma (§ 14) which in the Homeric age was nearly or
quite obsolete in the ordinary Ionic dialect; no trace of it
appears in the poems of Archilochus of Paros in the seventh

century B.C.   Aeolic forms are found in the Homeric poems
even where the metre does not require them, as ὀφέλλειεν
β 334 for ὀφείλειεν, ἐρεβεννή E 659 (ἐρεβεσ-νος), ἀργεννῆσι
Γ 141 (ἀργεσ-νος), φηρσίν A 268 for θηρσίν, φλίψεται ρ 221
for θλίψεται.   The general formulaic character of these Aeolisms indicates that they were borrowed from earlier poems
rather than from the Aeolians of the Homeric age.   Aeolic
form or coloring is found also in some proper names, as Θερσί-
της (found also in a Thessalian inscription of 214 B.C.), from
θέρσος the Aeolic form of θάρσος *insolence*, *daring*, Θερσίλο-
χος, Ἀλιθέρσης, Ναυσικάα (Ionic νηῦς), and perhaps θεά *goddess* (Ionic ἡ θεός).   Another Aeolic peculiarity is the use
of the smooth breathing as in ἦδος *pleasure* (*cf.* ἡδύς), ἄσμε-
νος *glad* (*cf.* ἀνδάνω, ἔαδον) ; see § 12 *m*.

g. Some forms seem to be borrowed from other dialects ;
but it must be remembered that when the poems were composed, there was less difference between the dialects than at
the earliest period when we have monumental evidence concerning them.   Thus the forms ἱππότα, μητίετα κτλ. (§ 16 *b*)
seem to be ancient rather than specifically Aeolic; that they
were not introduced simply *metri causa* is shown by the use
of νεφεληγερέτα Ζεύς A 511 where νεφεληγερέτης is metrically
admissible.

h. Some anomalies of form (as of verse) are as yet unexplained, but it may be assumed that all which remain either
(1) were justified by the usage of the people and might be
explained by more complete knowledge of the history of the
language, or (2) followed the analogy of what was in use, or
(3) are errors which have found their way into the text dur-
ing the course of transmission to the present time.   As the
poems were handed down among the Greeks at first orally,
and afterwards still uncritically for centuries, errors unavoid-
ably crept in and there was a gradual assimilation of what
was obsolete to later and more familiar forms, when the older
forms were unprotected by the metre.   ἐήνδανε γ 143 is prob-

ably an ancient assimilation to Attic usage for ἐάνδανε (ἐϜάν-
δανε, §§ 14, 25 *i*).

i. Doubtless also mistakes were committed in the process
of transferring the poems to the later alphabet (in official
use at Athens from the archonship of Euclides, 403 B.C.)
from the earlier alphabet in which E was used for ε, η, and
the spurious diphthong ει (which arises from compensative
lengthening or contraction, Hadley 14 b), and O was used
for ο, ω, and the spurious diphthong ου. Thus ΦΟΟΣ of the
old alphabet could be interpreted as φόος (the form intermediate between the earlier φάος and the Attic φῶς, as ποσσί
is intermediate between ποδ-σι and ποσί) or φόως, but the
latter form seemed more natural to those who said φῶς, and
it was introduced into the text, as B 49. ΕΟΣ might be ἧος
(or εἷος) or ἕως, but the latter as the familiar form is found
in the Mss., even A 193, where the metre demands the earlier
form; and εἵως is found where the rational form ἧος (or εἷος)
could stand. ΕΕΝ might be ἧεν, ἤην, ἔεν, ἔην. The last
form was thought to be "by διέκτασις" for ἦν (as ἐήν, the
possessive pronoun, for ἥν), and seems to have been often
substituted wrongly for ἔεν (§ 34 *g*). Since σπέους was the
Attic genitive of σπέος, σπείους seemed more natural than
σπεῖος (or σπέεος), as ὑπὸ σπείους· περὶ κτλ. ι 141 (see
§ 18 *n*). ἔρος Ξ 315 is protected by the metre, and is sus-
tained by the oblique cases ἔρῳ and ἔρον (§ 18 *e*), but the
Attic ἔρως has supplanted it in Γ 442, Ξ 294, where a consonant follows.

VOWELS AND VOWEL CHANGES.

§ 5. a. η is regularly used for ᾱ, as ἀγορή, ὁμοίη; except
in θεά *goddess*, λαός *people*, and some proper names (as
Αἰνείας, Ναυσικάα, § 4 *f*). Occasionally, as B 370, μάν is
found instead of the less frequent μήν (the strong form of
μέν). ἇλτο A 532 (from ἅλλομαι) is another instance of ᾱ,
unless it is to be written ἄλτο.

b. Sometimes, especially in abstract nouns, η represents Attic ᾰ, as εὐπλοΐην I 362, ἀληθείην η 297.

c. The final ᾱ of the stem is retained in the genitive endings -ᾱο and -ᾱων of the 1st declension, as Ἀτρείδαο A 203.

d. ᾱο is often changed to εω by transfer of quantity: Ἀτρείδαο, Ἀτρείδεω. *Cf.* βασιλῆος with Attic βασιλέως. But the frequent λᾱός never has the Attic form λεώς.

e. Compensative lengthening is sometimes found where it is not in Attic, as ξεῖνος (ξένϝος), εἵνεκα (Lesbian ἔννεκα), κούρη (κόρϝα), μοῦνος, οὖρος (ὄρϝος), δουρός. It is omitted in βόλεται Λ 319 (βούλεται, Aeolic βόλλεται, *cf.* βέλτιον); and in three compounds of πούς (ποδ-), as ἀελλόπος Θ 409.

A vowel seems to have been borrowed from the following syllable in χεῖρ, χειρός from a stem χερι-, and in πουλύς (Attic πολύς, § 20 *f*).

f. Diphthongs occasionally preserve ι where it is lost in Attic before a vowel: αἰεί, αἰετός, ἐτελείετο (§ 29 *i*), οἰνοβαρείων, ὀλοιή, πνοιή, χρύσειος. *Cf.* ἀκουή with Attic ἀκοή.

g. But ι is lost before a vowel in ὠκέα (ὠκεῖα) Ἶρις B 786, Αἰνέας N 541 (Αἰνείας, *cf.* κρείων with the proper names Κρέων and Κρέουσα), in -οο for -οιο as genitive-ending of the 2d declension (§ 17 *c*) and in ἐμέο for ἐμεῖο, etc. (§ 24 *e*); *cf.* μοῖρ' ὀλοή Φ 83 with ὀλοιὴ μοῖρα Χ 5, χρυσείοις A 246 with χρυσέῳ A 15. With these examples may be compared Attic ποεῖν (ποιεῖν), ἐλάα (ἐλαία). As in Attic, the penult is sometimes short in υἱός (as A 489, Δ 473) and οἷος (as η 312, Σ 105). *Cf.* ἔμπαῖον υ 379, χᾰμαϊευνάδες κ 243.

Cf. also the loss of υ in λόε κ 361 (ἔλουε), ἔχεαν Σ 347 (ἔχευαν), ἀλέασθε δ 774 (ἀλεύασθε), νήεσσι from νηύς, βασιλῆος from βασιλεύς, Τυδέος from Τυδεύς. See § 41 *o*. *Cf.* ἥρωος ζ 303.

h. ἑταῖρος (ἑταρ-ιος) is not a dialectic variation of ἔταρος but is derived from it as Αἰτώλιος Δ 399 from Αἰτωλός Δ 527, παννύχιος α 443 from πάννυχος Ψ 218. *Cf.* § 19 *b*.

§ 6. Contraction. a. Concurrent vowels generally remain uncontracted : ἀέκων, ἄλγεα, πάις (in nominative and vocative singular), ὄις (ὄϝις = *ovis, ewe*). Attic εὖ is regularly ἐύ before two consonants and the adjective is always ἐύς or ἠύς. Patronymics from nouns in -ευς form -εΐδης, -εΐων, as Ἀτρεΐδης Α 7, Πηλεΐωνα Α 197.

b. When contraction occurs, it follows the ordinary rules, except that εο and εου generally give ευ : θάρσευς Ρ 573, θέρευς η 118, φιλεῦντας γ 221 ; but ποντοπορούσης λ 11, ὁμοῦμαι Α 233.

c. εα are very rarely contracted into η, as Τυδῆ Δ 384 (Τυδέα), ἀκραῆ β 421, αἰνοπαθῆ σ 201.

d. ηε are contracted into η in τιμῆς Ι 605 (τιμήεις), τιμῆντα Σ 475, τεχνῆσσαι η 110 (τεχνήεσσαι).

e. ια are contracted into ι in ἀκοίτις κ 7 (ἀκοίτιας). ι and ε are contracted in ἱρά, as Β 420, and in ἵρηκες, as ε 66.

f. οε are contracted into ου in λωτοῦντα Μ 283.

g. οη are contracted into ω in ἐπιβώσομαι, as α 378, ὀγδώκοντα Β 568.

h. The optative-sign ι is sometimes lost in a preceding υ (§ 28 *b*).

i. It is probable that in the original form of the Homeric poems many vowels were uncontracted which are contracted in the Mss. and ordinary editions. The οι of κοῖλος can be pronounced as two syllables 67 times out of 68 (χ 385 being the exception). So αἰδοῖος may generally be αἰδόιος, and θεῖος may be θέιος (*cf.* § 4 *c*). The ει of Ἀργεῖος may always form two syllables. The evidence of rhythm and etymology indicates λόεσεν rather than λοῦσεν. See §§ 18 *l*, 29 *g*.

§ 7. Synizesis. a. Vowels which do not form a true diphthong may be blended in pronunciation into one long sound : Ἀτρεΐδεω ‿ ᴗ ᴗ ‿, θεοειδέα Γ 27, δὴ αὖτε Α 340, ἦ οὐκ ἀίεις α 298, μὴ ἄλλοι δ 165, πόλιος Β 811, Αἰγυπτίους δ 83, Ἱστίαιαν Β 537 (in which last three examples ι must have had

very nearly the pronunciation of its cognate *y*-sound, §§ 5 *g*,
41 *o γ*, as *omnia* is often disyllabic in Vergil), ὦ ἀρίγνωτε ρ 375.

The genitives in *-εω* are always pronounced with synizesis
(§ 16 *c*), as also ἡμέων and ὑμέων and regularly ἡμέας, σφέας,
and the genitive plural in *-εων* (§ 16 *d*). χρεώ is always a
monosyllable.

b. Synizesis often served the purpose of the later contraction: ἡμέων did not differ in metrical quantity from ἡμῶν.
It enabled the poet in certain cases to escape the combination _ ᴗ _ (*amphimacer*) which cannot be received unchanged into dactylic verse (§ 41 *a*).

c. Contraction and synizesis were employed in the last
foot of the verse more freely than elsewhere.

d. It is probable that in the original form of the poems
synizesis was not so common as in our texts; *e.g.* instead of
Πηληιάδεω Ἀχιλῆος A 1, Πηληιάδα *κτλ.* may have been
spoken. For ὑμῖν μὲν θεοὶ δοῖεν A 18, ὕμμι θεοὶ μὲν *κτλ.* has
been conjectured, and Ἐνναλίῳ βροτοφόντῃ for Ἐνναλίῳ ἀν-
δρεϊφόντῃ B 651. For δενδρέῳ ἐφεζόμενοι Γ 152, the Alexandrian scholar Zenodotus read δένδρει *κτλ.* (*cf.* the Attic
plural δένδρεσι). For Πηλείδη ἔθελ' A 277, probably Πηλείδη
θέλ' should be read, although the poet elsewhere uses ἐθέλω
not θέλω.

§ 8. CRASIS is not frequent. It is most common in compounds with πρό, as προύφαινε ι 145, προύχοντο γ 8, which
however may be written προέφαινε, προέχοντο *κτλ.* Note
also τούνεκα A 291, ὥριστος Ω 384 (ὁ ἄριστος), ωὑτός E 396,
τἄλλα γ 462, χἠμεῖς B 238 (καὶ ἡμεῖς), οὑμός Θ 360.

§ 9. HIATUS is allowed

a. After the vowels ι and υ, as ἔγχεϊ ὀξυόεντι E 50, τίς δὲ
σύ ἐσσι Z 123.

b. When the two vowels between which it occurs are sep-

arated by a caesura (καθῆστο ἐπιγνάμψασα A 569) or by a
diaeresis (§ 40 *h*): seldom (54 times) after the first foot
(αὐτὰρ ὁ ἔγνω A 333), more frequently (96 times) after the
fourth foot (ἔγχεα ὀξυόεντα E 568). This hiatus after the
fourth foot is more frequent in the Odyssey than in the Iliad.
Hiatus between the short syllables of the third foot is allowed nearly as frequently as in all other places together,
more than 200 times. This freedom of hiatus emphasizes
the prominence of this caesura, §§ 10 *e*, 40 *d*.

  c. When the final vowel of the first word is long and
stands in the accented part of the foot (§ 39 *c*), as τῷ σε
κακῇ αἴσῃ A 418. See § 41 *o* ζ.

  d. When a long vowel or diphthong loses part of its quantity before the following vowel (§ 41 *o*), as τὴν δ’ ἐγὼ οὐ
λύσω A 29, μή νύ τοι οὐ χραίσμῃ A 28. Here the final and
initial vowels may be said to be blended. This is called
weak or *improper* hiatus; it is essentially the same as the
following.

  e. When the last vowel of the first word is already elided,
as μυρί’ Ἀχαιοῖς ἄλγε’ ἔθηκεν A 2. See § 10 *e*.

  f. Hiatus before words which formerly began with a consonant (§§ 12 *l*, 14) is only apparent.

  g. The poet did not avoid two or more concurrent vowels
in the same word, § 6. But these vowels all seem to have
become concurrent on Greek soil by the loss of consonants.

  § 10. ELISION. **a.** ἄ (in inflectional endings and in ἄρα
and ῥά), ε, ἴ, ο may be elided. αι is sometimes elided in the
verb endings -μαι, -σαι (except in the infinitive), -ται, -σθαι,
and once in ὀξεῖαι Λ 272. οι is elided seven times in μοί,
three times in τοί, once in σοί A 170 (unless οὐδέ σοι οἴω or
οὔ σοι ὀίω should be read there for οὐδέ σ’ ὀίω).

  b. τό, πρό, ἀντί, περί, τί, and the conjunction ὅτι do not
suffer elision; ὅτ’ is for ὅτε (either the temporal conjunction
or the relative ὅ with τέ affixed, § 24 *q*), τ’ for τέ or τοί.

  c. ι is seldom elided in the dative singular, where it seems
originally to have been long.

d. Oxytone prepositions and conjunctions lose their accent
in elision; other oxytones throw the acute accent upon the
preceding syllable: κατ' ἄρ' ἔζετο Α 101, but λεύκ' ὀστέα
a 161, εἴμ' Ὀδυσεύς ι 19.

e. Elision tends to unite the two words between which
it occurs; hence it is avoided at the caesura of the third
foot, where hiatus seems to be preferred to elision.   Hence,
also, the poet does not avoid the hiatus which sometimes
remains after elision, § 9 e, g.

f. Elision is not left to the reader as in Latin poetry.   In
the best Ms. of the Iliad (*Ven. A*), the elided vowel was
sometimes written over the preceding consonant, and where
the elided vowel bore the accent, a *grave* accent was placed
over the preceding vowel.

§ **11.** APOCOPE. **a.** Before a consonant, the short final
vowel of ἄρα and of the prepositions ἀνά, κατά, παρά, may
be cut off (ἀποκοπή, ἀποκόπτω).   The accent is then thrown
back upon the preceding syllable (although it might be more
rational to consider it lost as it is in elision).

b. After apocope, the ν of ἀνά and τ of κατά follow the
usual rules for consonant changes: ἀγκρεμάσασα a 440, ἀμπεπαλών Γ 355, ἀλλέξαι Φ 321 (ἀναλέξαι), ἀγξηράνῃ Φ 347
(ἀναξηράνῃ), κάββαλεν Ε 343 (κατέβαλεν), κὰδ δέ (κατὰ δέ)
frequently, κάλλιπε λ 279, κάκτανε Ζ 164 (κατέκτανε), καπ-
πεσέτην Ε 560, καρρέζουσα Ε 424, καστορνῦσα ρ 32 (κατα-
στορνῦσα), κὰπ φάλαρα Π 106.

c. ἀπό suffers apocope in ἀππέμψει ο 83; *cf.* Latin *ab*.

d. ὑπό suffers apocope in ὑββάλλειν Τ 80; *cf.* Latin *sub*.

e. αὐέρυσαν Α 459 is explained as derived by apocope, assimilation, and vocalization of ϝ, from ἀνά and ϝερύω: ἀνϝ-
ρυσαν, ἀϝερυσαν, αὐέρυσαν, *cf.* καυάξαις Hesiod *Works* 666
(καταϝάξαις).   For this apocope *cf.* κάσχεθε (κατέσχεθε) Λ
702, and ἀμνάσει Pindar *Pyth.* IV 54 (ἀναμνήσει); for the
vocalization of ϝ, see § 14 *j*.

f. Apocope was no mere metrical license; it seems to have been common in the conversational idiom of some dialects. A Megarian peasant is made to say (Aristophanes *Acharnians* 732) ἄμβατε πὸτ τὰν μᾶδδαν for ἀνάβατε ποτί (πρὸς) τὴν μᾶζαν, where the poet is certainly imitating the manner of the common people. ἀμβώσας (ἀναβοήσας) is found in Herodotus I 8, ἀμπαύεσθαι Hdt. I 182, ἀμβολάδην Hdt. IV 181. More striking examples of apocope and assimilation than any in Homer are found in prose inscriptions, as ἀτ τᾶς for ἀπὸ τῆς, ἐτ τοῖ for ἐπὶ τοῦ, πὸκ κί for ποτὶ κί (πρὸς τί), πὲρ τοῦννεουν (§ 24 *m*) for περὶ τῶνδεων, in a Thessalian inscription of 214 B.C., found at Larissa. *Cf.* πὸτ τὸν θεὸν κὰτ πάτρια διδόντων in a Delphian inscription of 380 B.C. Apocope was the rule in the Thessalian and Boeotian dialects.

CONSONANTS AND CONSONANT CHANGES.

§ 12. a. Where collateral forms appear, one with single and the other with doubled consonants, the form with two consonants is generally the older or justified etymologically, as ποσσί, ποσί (from ποδ-σι); νείκεσσε, νείκεσε (νεῖκος, νεικεσ-), ὅππως (ὅκϝως, *cf.* Latin *quis etc.*), ὅττι, κτλ.

b. Single initial consonants, especially λ, μ, ν, ρ, σ, are often doubled (as ρ is in Attic) when by inflexion or composition a short vowel is brought before them (see § 41 *j a*), as ἐλλίσσετο Ζ 45, ἔμμαθον, ἐύννητος, ἔσσυο, ὅππως, ὅττι.

c. But sometimes ρ is not doubled where it would be in Attic, as ἔρεξα δ 352 (§ 25 *g*), ἄρεκτον Τ 150, ὠκυρόῳ Ε 598, θυμοραϊστέων Σ 220.

d. Palatal and lingual mutes often remain unchanged before μ, as ἀκαχμένος, ὀδμήν, ἴδμεν, κεκορυθμένος.

e. Lingual mutes are commonly assimilated to a following σ, as ποσσί (ποδ-σι). σ is sometimes assimilated to μ or ν: ἔμμεναι (εἶναι) for ἐσ-μεναι, ἔννεπε *a* 1 *tell* for ἐν-σεπε (Lat.

insece), ἀργεννός *white* for ἀργεσ-νος, as ἀργεννάων Γ 19ε, ἕννυμι for ϝεσ-νυμι (§ 14 *a*) *cf.* ἔσσα δ 253, ἐραννήν η 18 *lovely*,
ἐρεβεννή Ε 659 *dark*, *cf.* Ἔρεβος.   *Cf.* the aorist ὀφέλλειεν
β 334 for ὀφελσειεν.   See § 4 *f*.

f. σ is frequently retained before σ, as ἔσσομαι, ἐτέλεσσε.

g. Between μ and λ or ρ, β is sometimes developed (*cf.*
the Attic μεσημβρία from μέση ἡμέρα, and *chamber* with Latin
camera), as ἄμβροτος from stem μρο or μορ (Latin *mors*,
morior), while in βροτός *mortal* and νὺξ ἀβρότη Ξ 78, the μ
of the stem is lost; μέμβλωκε from μλο or μολ (*cf.* ἔμολον),
while in προβλώσκειν φ 239, the μ of the stem is lost; μέμ-
βλετο Φ 516 from μέλω ι 20; ἤμβροτον Π 336 (*cf.* ἅμαρτε
ζ 116 and ἀβροτάξομεν Κ 65).

h. κάμβαλε is found occasionally, as ζ 172, in the Mss. as
a variant reading, a softer pronunciation for κάββαλε (§ 11 *b*).

i. A parasitic τ appears in πτόλις, πτόλεμος for πόλις, πόλεμος.   *Cf.* διχθά, τριχθά with Attic δίχα, τρίχα, — χθαμα-
λός (*humilis*) with χαμαί (*humi*). The form πτόλις is found
in Thessalian and Cyprian inscriptions, and was also Arcadian.   The proper names *Neoptolemus* (Νεοπτόλεμος) and
Ptolemy (Πτολεμαῖος) preserved this τ to a late period.
Τληπτόλεμος is found in an ancient Boeotïan inscription; in
this word τ could not have been inserted *metri causa*.

j. Certain words were losing their initial consonants in
the Homeric age: *cf.* μικρός γ 296 with σμικρῇσι Ρ 757, ὕες
ο 556 with σῦς τ 439, κεδασθέντες Β 398 with σκέδασεν Ρ 649,
ξυνιόντες Δ 446 with συνίτην Ζ 120, δούπησεν Δ 504 with
ἐγδούπησαν Λ 45 and ἐριδούπῳ γ 399 with ἐρίγδουπος Η 411.

k. For ϝ see § 14.

l. Yod (*j* pronounced as *y*) occasionally retains the force
of a consonant in ἵημι (§ 25 *h*) and generally (37 times) in
postpositive ὥς *i.e.* ϳώς (§ 41 *m*), which seldom leaves the preceding syllable short. The constant position of ὡς after the
noun which it qualifies marks the lengthening as a relic of
an earlier age. But perhaps this postpositive ὥς was ϝώς.

m. The *rough breathing* (*h*) has no power to prevent elision or weaken hiatus. The smooth breathing is found with several words which have the rough breathing in Attic, as ἄμμες (ἡμεῖς), ἦμαρ (ἡμέρα), ἆλτο (from ἄλλομαι), ἠέλιος (ἥλιος), Ἀΐδης (Ἀΐδης), ἠώς (ἕως). See § 4 *f.*

n. The ν movable was written by some ancient critics (*e.g.* Aristarchus) after the ending -ει of the pluperfect, as βεβλήκειν E 661, ἠνώγειν Z 170 ; *cf.* ἤσκειν Γ 388 (ἤσκεεν). It is freely used before consonants to make a syllable long by position (§ 41 *h*).

o. The final σ of adverbs is omitted more often than in prose ; not merely ἐξ and ἐκ, οὕτως and οὕτω, but also πώς and πώ, πολλάκις and πολλάκι (and similar adverbs in -κις, even with elision, τοσσάχ' ὕδωρ ἀπολέσκετ' λ 586), ἀτρέμας and ἀτρέμα, μεσσηγύς and μεσσηγύ, μέχρις and μέχρι, ἄχρις and ἄχρι, ἀμφίς and ἀμφί (adverbial), are found as collateral forms.

§ 13. METATHESIS of α and ρ is frequent : καρδίη B 452, κραδίη α 353 ; θάρσος α 321, θράσος (once) Ξ 416 (while the adjective is always θρασύς) ; κάρτος δ 415 (κάρτιστοι A 266), κράτος A 509. *Cf.* ἔδρακον from δέρκομαι, ἔδραθον from δαρθάνω, ἔπραθον from πέρθω, τραπείομεν Γ 441 from τέρπω, τερπικέραυνος from τρέπω.

For the shifting of quantity from -άο to -εω, see § 5 *d.*

§ 14. THE DIGAMMA. **a.** The following words seem to have been pronounced by the Homeric poet more or less consistently with initial digamma (*vau*, ϝ, pronounced as English *w*) : —

ἄγνυμι *break*, as E 161 ; *cf.* ἔαξα, ἀαγές λ 575.

ἅλις *enough*, as ν 136, B 90.

ἁλῶναι *be captured*, as M 172 ; *cf.* ἑάλων, Aeolic εὐάλωκεν (see *j* below). Also εἴλω *press*, as Π 403, from the same root.

ἄναξ *king*, as A 7 and often.

ἀνδάνω *please*, as β 114 ; *cf.* ἔαδον and ἐήνδανε [ἐάνδανε] γ 143.

ἀραιός *thin*, as Σ 411.

ἀρνός *lamb*, as Δ 158.

ἄστυ *city*, as Γ 245 and often.

ἕ, οὗ, οἷ *him etc.*, as A 510, with the possessive pronoun ὅς, ἥ, ὅν (ἑός κτλ.) ; see *h* below.

ἔαρ *Spring*, as τ 519 ; *cf.* Latin *ver.*

ἕδνα *wedding-gifts*, as X 472, perhaps from the same root as ἀνδάνω.

ἔθνος *tribe*, as ξ 73.

εἴκοσι *twenty*, as B 510 ; *cf.* Latin *viginti.*

εἴκω *yield*, as ὑποείκειν Υ 266 ; *cf.* English *weak, weaken.*

εἴρω *say*, future ἐρέω, as Δ 182 ; *cf.* Latin *ver-bum*, English *word.*

ἑκάς *far*, as E 791 ; *cf.* μέλποντές ἑκάεργον A 474.

ἕκαστος *each*, as B 449.

ἑκυρός *father-in-law*, as Γ 172 ; *cf.* German *Schwiegervater.*

ἑκών *willing*, as Z 523 ; *cf.* ἀέκων, ἀέκητι, ἀεκαζόμενος.

ἕλιξ *winding*, as α 92.

ἐλπίς, ἔλπομαι, *hope*, as π 101 ; *cf.* ἔολπα, ἀελπτέοντες.

ἕννυμι (Ϝεσ-νυμι), ἐσθής, εἵματα, *clothes*, as Γ 392 ; *cf.* Latin *vestis.*

ἔπος *word*, as Λ 652 ; *cf.* ἔειπον (ἐ-Ϝε-Ϝεπον, § 25 *h*), and ὄψ with Latin *vox.*

ἔργον, ἔρδω *work*, as B 436 ; *cf.* the English word.

ἐρύω, ἔρρω, *draw, go*, as δ 367 ; *cf.* ἀπόερσε.

ἕσπερος *evening*, as ρ 191 ; *cf.* Latin *vesper.*

ἔτος *year*, as α 16 ; *cf.* Latin *vetus.*

ἕξ *six*, as E 270.

ἔτης *companion*, as H 295.

ἡδύς *sweet*, as Δ 17 ; *cf.* ἀνδάνω and Latin *suadeo, suavis* (*suadvis*).

ἦθος *haunt*, as ξ 411 ; *cf.* εἴωθε.

ἰάχω *cry aloud* as δ 454 ; *cf. j* below.

ἰδεῖν *see*, as A 262 ; also οἶδα, εἶδος. *Cf.* Latin *video*, English *wit.*

ἴκελος, ἔοικα *am like*, as A 119.

ἴον *violet*, as ε 72 ; *cf.* Latin *viola.*

ἴς, ἶφι *strength, sinew*, as Ψ 191 ; *cf.* Latin *vis.*

ἴσος *equal*, as A 163 ; *cf.* ἔϊσος.

ἴτυς *felly*, as Δ 486 ; *cf.* English *withe.*

οἶκος *house*, as α 232 ; *cf.* Latin *vicus*, English *War-wick*, *Ber-wick*, etc.

οἶνος *wine*, as Γ 300 ; *cf.* Latin *vinum* and the English word.

b. It is probable that ἦρα (ἐπὶ ἦρα φέρων Α 572), Ἴλιος, and Ἴρις also were pronounced with initial ϝ.

c. ἀνδάνω, ἕ, ἕκυρος, ἕξ and others seem to have begun originally with two consonants, σϝ.

d. The verse alone affords no sufficient criterion for the former existence of ϝ in any word; it only indicates the loss of some consonant. This is not conclusive evidence for ϝ, since σ and *j* (*y*) were also lost. Which consonant originally was present has to be learned in each case from inscriptions of other Greek dialects, from a few notes of ancient grammarians, and from other cognate languages (*cf.* ἔργον *work*, οἶνος *wine*).

Rem. The Alexandrian scholars did not know of the existence of ϝ in the Homeric language, and consequently they did not use it to explain peculiarities in the Homeric text. The great English scholar Richard Bentley (1662–1742) was the first to discover that its restoration removed many difficulties of Homeric prosody.

e. The sound of ϝ evidently was going out of use in the Homeric period; it is not infrequently neglected in our texts and sometimes this neglect seems to be due to the poet himself, but ϝ can be restored in many passages by minor changes : κεδνὰ ἰδυῖα (ϝιδυῖα) has been restored for the Ms. reading κέδν᾽ εἰδυῖα α 428. For υἱὸν ἑκηβόλον Α 21 it is possible to read υἷα ϝεκηβόλον, for ἡβήσῃ τε καὶ ἧς κτλ. α 41 it is easy to read ἡβήσῃ καὶ ϝῆς, and πᾶσιν δὲ ϝανάσσειν for πάντεσσι δ᾽ ἀνάσσειν Α 288. For ἑπτάετες δ᾽ ἤνασσε γ 304, ἑπτάετες δ᾽ ἐάνασσε may be read (§ 25 *i*). μένος θυμόν τε ϝεκάστου may have been the original form of μένος καὶ θυμὸν ἑκάστου Ε 470. αὐτοὺς δὲ ἑλώρια Α 4 became αὐτοὺς δ᾽ ἑλώρια in many Mss. οἳ μὲν οἶνον α 110 is now read where the

Mss. have οἱ μὲν ἄρ᾽ οἶνον. As the Alexandrian grammarians
and the copyists had no knowledge of this lost letter in
Homer, they were solicitous to fill each hiatus by a ν movable, ῥ᾽ (ῥά), τ᾽ (τέ), γ᾽ (γέ), or whatever other addition or
change suggested itself. οὐ σύ γ᾽ ἄγεις ρ 576 is probably
for οὐ σύ ϝ (ϝε) ἄγεις, and ὃς ἄξει Ω 154 for ὅς ϝ ἄξει
(§ 41 *q*).

f. ϝ was less constantly preserved in derivative than in
primitive words: οἶνος generally retains its ϝ, but Οἰνόμαος
E 706 has lost it; ἀρνός preserves its ϝ four times, but ἀρνειός
shows no trace of it.

g. It has been computed that ϝ in Homer assists in mak-
ing position 359 times (only in the accented part of the foot
or else before the third personal pronoun — before εὖ once,
before the enclitic οἷ 39 times), but prevents hiatus 2995
times (2324 of which are after a short syllable, in the unaccented part of the foot). The force of ϝ is neglected about
600 times in ordinary texts (about half of which passages
can be readily changed to restore ϝ).

h. In later poets, *e.g.* in the elegiac poets and Pindar, ϝ
seems never to make position but often prevents hiatus, —
poetic precedent allowing hiatus before a word which formerly began with ϝ. The consciousness of the consonantal
initial sound of οἷ was retained longest and most clearly.
Before that word, no attempt was made to fill a hiatus by ν
movable or by οὐχ for οὐ, and before it a short vowel was
often long by position (§ 41 *m*).

i. That the sound of ϝ was still alive in the Homeric age
is shown by the accuracy of the poet in its use where comparative philology shows that it once existed.

j. ϝ sometimes leaves a trace of its existence in its cognate
vowel υ: εὔαδεν Ξ 340 for ἔϝαδεν, ἀνέρυσαν A 459 for ἀϝέρυ-
σαν (§ 11 *e*), αὐίαχοι N 41 for ἀϝίαχοι (a privative and ϝια-
χή), ταλαύρινον E 289 for ταλά-ϝρινον. So doubtless ἀπούρας
A 356 for ἀπο-ϝράς. *Cf.* the Pindaric ἀϝάταν, *Pyth.* II 28,

for ἀϝάταν, and εὔιδον Sappho II 7 for ἔϝιδον. This latter
εὔιδον may have been pronounced often where our Homeric
texts have εἴσιδον, as ἔσιδεν seems not infrequently to have
been substituted for ἔϝιδεν.

Some irregularities of quantity may be explained by this
vocalization of ϝ. Thus ἀπὄειπών Τ 35 may have been ἀπο-
ϝειπών pronounced nearly as ἀπονειπών. αὐίαχοι finds its
analogy in γένετο ἰαχή Δ 456 (γένετονιαχή).

k. A neighboring vowel is sometimes lengthened to com-
pensate for the loss of ϝ (§ 41 d).

l. An ε was sometimes prefixed to a digammated word and
remained after the ϝ was lost, as ἐέλδωρ, ἐείκοσι, ἐέργει, ἐέ.

m. Sometimes the rough breathing represents the last
remnant of a lost consonant (especially in the words which
once began with σϝ, as ἀνδάνω κτλ., cf. c above), as ἑκών,
ἕσπερος. Often the same root varies in breathing, as ἀνδάνω
and ἡδύς, but ἦδος, — ἕννυμι, but ἐσθής.

n. For the augment and reduplication of digammated
verbs, see § 25 h.

o. For δϝείδω, δϝήν, see § 41, j β.

DECLENSION.

§ 15. SPECIAL CASE ENDINGS. **a.** The suffix -φι(ν), a
remnant of an old instrumental case, added to the stem forms
a genitive and dative in both singular and plural. It is generally used as an instrumental, ablative, or locative case.
The suffix is most frequent in set expressions and in the last
two feet of the verse.

1st Declension, always singular: ἐξ εὐνῆφιν *from the couch*,
ἦφι βίηφι *with his own might*, θύρηφι *at the door*.

2d Declension: ἐκ ποντόφιν *out of the sea*, δακρυόφι *with
tears*, ἐπ᾽ ἐσχαρόφιν *on the hearth*. The final ο of the stem
always receives the acute accent.

3d Declension, only with σ stems except ναῦφι and κοτυ-
ληδονόφι (which has gone over into the 2d declension), and

always plural except κράτεσφι Κ 156: ἐκ στήθεσφιν *from the breasts,* ὄρεσφιν *on the mountains.*

b. Many of these forms are found only where they are convenient for the verse; *e.g.* ναῦφι always stands for νηῶν, not for νηυσί which has the same metrical form as ναῦφι.

c. This ending is not used with designations of persons, except αὐτόφι Τ 255, Υ 140, θεόφιν as Η 366.

d. The suffix -θι is added to the stem to denote *place where:* θύρηθι *at the door,* οἴκοθι *at home,* κηρόθι *at heart,* πόθι *where,* κεῖθι *there* (ἐκεῖ is not Homeric), ἠῶθι *in the morning.*

e. The suffix -θεν is added to the stem to denote *place whence:* Ἴδηθεν *from Ida,* οὐρανόθεν *from heaven.* It forms a genitive with the pronominal stems ἐμε, σε, ἑ, αὐτο: ἐμέθεν, σέθεν, ἕθεν, αὐτόθεν. Sometimes a preposition is used with it, as ἐξ ἀλόθεν Φ 335, ἀπὸ Τροίηθεν ι 38, ἔθεν εἵνεκα Γ 128, πρὸ ἔθεν Ε 96. When affixed to adverbial stems, it may lose its final ν: ὄπισθε, ἄνευθε, πάροιθε, ἔνερθε.

f. This ending -θεν has lost its original force in certain adverbs; ἐγγύς, ἐγγύθι, ἐγγύθεν do not differ essentially in meaning; *cf.* ἔνδον, ἔνδοθι, ἔνδοθεν, — πρόσθεν, ὄπισθεν, κτλ. The Aeolic form of the ending appears in ὕπαιθα Φ 493 *from under.*

g. The enclitic -δε is added to the accusative to denote more distinctly the limit of motion: οἰκόνδε *homeward* (also οἴκαδε, especially of the return of the Achaeans to their homes) ὄνδε δόμονδε *to his own house,* ἅλαδε *seaward,* κλισίηνδε *to the tent,* Τροίηνδε *to Troy.* So also Ἀϊδόσδε *to the abode of Hades; cf.* ἡμετερόνδε (*sc.* δῶμα) *to our house,* εἰς Ἀΐδαο. With Πηλειωνάδε Ω 338, *cf.* εἰς Ἀγαμέμνονα Η 312. *Cf.* -δις in ἄλλυδις, ἄμυδις, χαμάδις, -ζε in ἔραζε *to the earth,* θύραζε, χαμᾶζε. φύγαδε *to flight* (for φύγηνδε which is not used) is formed as from a noun of the third declension.

§ 16. First Declension. **a.** η is found for final α of the stem with the exceptions mentioned in § 5 *a* f.

b. The nominative singular of some masculines ends in
-τᾰ for -της : αἰχμητά *spearman*, μητίετα *counsellor*.　*Cf.* the
Latin *poetă, naută*.　εὐρύοπα *far-sounding* (perhaps a petrified
nominative) is used also as accusative, *e.g.* A 498.

All of these words are adjectival (*titular*) except Θυέστα
B 107.

c. The genitive singular of masculines ends in -ᾱο or (by
transfer of quantity, § 5 *d*), -εω.　After a vowel this ending
may be contracted to -ω : ἐυμμελίω Δ 47, Αἰνείω Ε 534, Βορέω
Ψ 692.　The ending -εω is always pronounced as one syllable
by synizesis (§ 7).

d. The genitive plural ends in -αων or -εων : θεάων, βου-
λέων.　After ι this ending may be contracted, as παρειῶν Ω
794.　After a long syllable (*i.e.* everywhere except in πυλέων
Η 1, Μ 340, and θυρέων φ 191) synizesis of -εων occurs, as
ναυτέων.

e. The dative plural ends in -ῃσι(ν) or rarely in -ῃς, as
θύρῃσιν, πέτρῃς, — in -αις only in three words : θεαῖς ε 119
(*cf.* θεά § 5 *a*), ἀκταῖς Μ 284, πάσαις χ 471.

f. The short form of this dative ending is rarely used
before a consonant ; when it stands before a vowel, it may
be said that the final ι has been elided.

§ 17. SECOND DECLENSION.　**a.** The genitive singular
has preserved the old ending -ιο which affixed to the stem
vowel makes -οιο.

b. According to tradition this ending does not suffer elision ; but elision is metrically possible, *e.g.* δυσομένου Ὑπερίονος α 24 might be δυσομένοι᾽ Ὑπερίονος.　See § 7 *d*.

c. The termination -οο is indicated by the metre in certain
places where all the Mss. give a corrupt form : ὀψιτέλεστον
ὅο κλέος οὔ ποτ᾽ ὀλεῖται Β 325, Πολύφημον ὅο κράτος ἐστὶ μέ-
γιστον α 70, ἀδελφεόο φρένας ἥρως Η 120, Ἰλίοο προπάροιθε
Χ 6, Αἰόλοο μεγαλήτορος κ 36.　It is to be recognized also
in Πετεῶο Β 552 for Πετεάοο, from Πετεῶς for Πετεάος.　It

was probably far more common in the original form of the poems; e.g. Ὀλυμπίου ἀθρόοι a 27 might be Ὀλυμπίο’ ἀθρόοι. The Attic ending -ου is more common in the received texts.

For the loss of ι in the change from -οιο to οο, see § 5 g.

d. The genitive and dative dual end in -οιιν: τοῖιν, ὤμοιιν.

e. The dative plural ends in -οισι(ν) or -οις. As in the first declension (§ 16 f) the long ending is the rule, the short ending is very rare before a consonant.

f. γαλόῳ Χ 473 (nom. pl.), Ἀθόω Ξ 229 (gen. sing.), and Κόων Ξ 255 (acc. sing.) belong to the so-called Attic Second Declension. But Homer uses λαός, νηός, κάλος, λαγωός for λεώς, νεώς, κτλ.

§ 18. THIRD DECLENSION. a. The ending ι of the dative singular is sometimes long, as in Latin, and sometimes short. It is seldom elided. It is often long before a single consonant, as κνήστι χαλκείῃ Λ 640, μήτι δ’ ἡνίοχος Ψ 318; it is always long in διΐφιλος, Διὶ μῆτιν ἀτάλαντος, cf. ὑπερμενεῖ φίλον Β 116, κράτεΐ γε Η 142. So before words which once began with ϝ, as ἀνδρὶ ἰκέλη Δ 86, τέκεϊ ᾧ δ 175; cf. Διὶ ὥς Β 781 (§ 12 l). It preserves its length before a vowel in ἐν δέπαϊ ὄφρα Ω 285.

b. The genitive and dative dual are very rare; perhaps only ποδοῖιν Ψ 770, Σειρήνοιιν μ 52, 167.

c. The dative plural has the Aeolic ending -εσσι(ν) as well as the Attic -σι(ν): πόδεσσι, ποσσί (§ 12 e), ποσί, — βελέεσσι (for βελεσ-εσσι), βέλεσσι, βέλεσι, — ἄνδρεσσι, ἀνδράσι, — θυγατέρεσσι (Attic θυγατράσι), — κλαιόντεσσι (Attic κλαίουσι), — κύνεσσι, κυσί. σπέσσι from σπέος is irregular; it can be written everywhere σπέεσι. Sometimes -σσι is used after a vowel, νέκυσσι as well as νεκύεσσι. As the examples show, sometimes one σ is dropped, but -εσι for -εσσι (as ἀνάκτεσιν ο 557) is not frequent. The forms in -εσσι are always accented on the antepenult.

d. Forms with -εσσι have replaced occasionally in the Mss. forms with -σι, as θέλγεσκ᾽ ἐπέεσσιν γ 264 for θέλγεσκε ϝέπεσσιν (§ 14 *a*, *e*), ἀγανοῖς βελέεσσιν γ 280 for ἀγανοῖσι βέλεσσιν (§ 17 *e*).

e. γέλως, ἔρως, ἴδρως have no stems with τ, but form dat. γέλῳ, ἔρῳ, ἴδρῳ, acc. γέλω (or γέλον), ἔρον, ἴδρω. χρώς has χροός, χροΐ, χρόα, but also χρωτός Κ 575, χροιῇ Ξ 164, χρῶτα σ 172.

f. γόνυ, δεσμός, δόρυ, κάρη, οὖς (which probably should be written ὄας, from οὖας), πρόσωπον all have forms from τ-stems: γούνατος (γουνός Λ 547, τ 450), γούνασι, δέσματα, δούρατος, δούρατι, δούρατα, δούρασι κτλ.- κάρη has four sets of inflexions: (1) κάρητος, κάρητι,— (2) καρήατος, καρήατι, καρήατα, — (3) κράατος, κράατι, κράατα, — (4) κρατός, κρατί, κράτα, κράτων, κρασίν. κρῆθεν is used as its genitive Π 548, κάρ as accusative singular Π 392. All the oblique cases of οὖς are formed from the stem οὐατ-, except ὠσίν μ 200.

πρόσωπον has προσώπατα σ 192, προσώπασι Η 212.

g. Several stems in -ιδ form the accusative singular in -α; γλαυκώπιδα Θ 373, γλαυκῶπιν α 156 ; ἀνάλκιδα Θ 153, ἄναλκιν γ 375, ἔριδα Ε 861, ἔριν γ 136. *Cf.* μάστιγα Ε 226, μάστιν ο 182, Attic ὄρνιθα, ὄρνιν.

h. Nouns in -ηρ have both syncopated and unsyncopated forms: πατρός, πατέρος (πατρῶν δ 687), ἀνδρός, ἀνέρος.

i. Nouns in -ος and -ας generally remain uncontracted. -εος is rarely contracted to -ευς, as θάρσευς Ρ 573 (Ὀδυσεὺς ω 398). *Cf.* ἀκραῆ (ἀκραέα) β 421, Διομήδεα Δ 365.

j. The α of a few stems in -ας is weakened to ε: οὔδεος, οὔδεϊ from οὖδας, κώεσιν from κῶας *fleece.* In the plural the final α is short in γέρα, as Β 237.

k. Forms of κλέος and adjectives in -κλῆς are contracted in the Mss.: κλέα ἀνδρῶν Ι 189, εὐκλείας Κ 281, δυσκλέα Β 115, ἀκλέα δ 728; *cf.* ὑπερδέα Ρ 330.

l. It is probable that the true reading is κλέε᾽ ἀνδρῶν (the trisyllabic can everywhere be substituted for the anomalous disyllabic form), δυσκλέε᾽ Ἄργος, ἀκλέε᾽ ἐκ μεγάρων.

m. Proper names compounded with κλέος are inflected thus: N. βίη Ἡρακληείη (periphrasis for Ἡρακλέης which is metrically impossible, § 2 *s*), G. Ἡρακλῆος, D. Ἡρακλῆι, A. Ἡρακλῆα.

n. Probably the η or ει of the nouns in -ος and -ας should be resolved: σπείους may always be written σπέεος, σπήεσσι may be σπεέεσσι (σπεεσ-εσσι, see *c* above), δείους may be δέεος, ἐυρρεῖος may be ἐυρρεέος, κρειῶν may be κρεάων, ἀγακλῆος may be ἀγακλέεος, ἀκλείως may be ἀκλεέως, Ἡρακλῆος may always be Ἡρακλέεος, etc. See § 6 *i*.

o. Nouns in -ω and -ως are contracted in the Mss. This may be a conformation to Attic usage. Generally it is possible, and often it is rhythmically better, to write *e.g.* ἠόα δῖαν rather than ἠῶ δῖαν (§ 39 *j*).

p. Nouns in -ις and -υς usually retain ι or υ throughout, but in its stead may insert ε which is sometimes lengthened.

q. πόλις is inflected thus: πόλιος, πόληος, πόλει, πόληϊ Γ 50, πόλιν, πόλιες, πόληες, πολίων πολίεσσι, πόλιας, πόληας (ρ 486), πόλεις.

r. Nouns in -ευς generally lengthen ε to η in compensation (§ 41 *d*) for the υ which between two vowels becomes ϝ and is lost, as βασιλεύς, βασιλῆος. Forms with ε are found in proper names: Τυδέος Β 406, Τυδέα Ζ 222, Ὀδυσεύς ω 398 (once) for Ὀδυσέος.

s. νηῦς (Attic ναῦς) is inflected thus: νηός, νεός, νηΐ, νῆα (νέα only ι 283 and doubtful), νῆες, νέες, νηῶν, νεῶν, ναῦφι, νήεσσι, νέεσσι, νηυσί, νῆας, νέας. The forms with η are the most frequent.

t. Ἄρης has Ἄρη and Ἄρην (Ε 909) of the first declension; and Ἄρηος, Ἄρηι, Ἄρηα as from Ἄρευς (the Lesbian form of Ἄρης, *cf.* the Attic genitive Ἄρεως). With these latter forms may be compared conversely the dialectic collateral forms in -ης of Epic proper names in -ευς, as Ὀρφης (Ὀρφεύς), Τύδης (Τυδεύς), from which were borrowed the Latin *Ulixēs*, *Achillēs*, etc.

ANOMALOUS FORMS.

§ 19. a. As verbs appear in the present system with a variety of collateral forms derived from the same root (*cf.* ἴκω, ἱκάνω, ἱκνέομαι,— πεύθομαι, πυνθάνομαι, — μένω, μίμνω, μιμνάζω), so nouns of different declensions are sometimes formed from the same root and are used without appreciable difference of meaning.

b. Some nouns have both vowel and consonant stems: ἀλκή Γ 45, but ἀλκί Ε 299; ἄστρα Θ 555, but ἀστήρ Ζ 295; γάστρην Σ 348, but γαστήρ ζ 133; ἐγχείη Η 261, but ἔγχος Η 254; ἐρίηρος ἑταῖρος Δ 266, but ἐρίηρες ἑταῖροι Γ 378; ἡνίοχος Λ 280, but ἡνιοχῆες Ε 505; ἰωκή Ε 740, but ἰῶκα Λ 601; φυλακούς Ω 566, but φύλακας Κ 97; *cf.* Attic πατροφόνος with πατροφονῆα α 299, πολυδακρύου Ρ 192 (for which however πολυδάκρυος is conjectured) as genitive of πολύδακρυς (*cf.* δακρυό-εις Χ 499) with πολύδακρυν Γ 132, πολιήτας Β 806 with πολῖται η 131.

c. μάστι Ψ 500 and μάστιν ο 182 are collateral with μάστιγι Ε 748 and μάστιγα Ε 226; so also verbs are found from both stems: μάστιε Ρ 622, μάστιξεν Ε 366.

d. Of υἱός, three stems are found: (1) υἱός, υἱόν, υἱέ. The other forms of this declension are very rare; υἱοῦ χ 238, υἱῷ Π 177. (2) υἱέος, υἱέϊ, υἱέα (only Ν 350 in Homer, frequent in later poets) κτλ., as if from υἱύς which occurs on Spartan and Arcadian inscriptions, with ὑύς on an early Athenian inscription. (3) υἷος, υἷι, υἷα, υἷε, υἷες, υἱάσι, υἷας, as from a nominative υἷς.

In this word the first syllable is sometimes short (§ 5 *g*), as it often is in Attic and in other dialects.

e. So also some proper names have forms of both vowel and consonant stems: Αἰθιοπῆας Α 423 and Αἰθίοπας α 23; Ἀντιφατῆα κ 114 and Ἀντιφάτης ο 243; Πατροκλῆος, Πατροκλῆα, Πατρόκλεις, as well as Πάτροκλος, Πατρόκλου κτλ.

f. Ἀΐδης has Ἀΐδαο, Ἀΐδεω, but also Ἄϊδος, Ἄϊδι as if

from Ἄϊς (Ἀϊδ-).   Cf. Οἰδιπόδαο λ 271 with the Attic genitive Οἰδίποδ-ος.   A collateral form of Ἀΐδης is Ἀϊδωνεύς
Υ 61 with dative Ἀϊδωνῆι Ε 190.

g. Ζεύς has Ζηνός, Ζηνί, Ζῆνα, or, at end of the verse, Ζῆν,
as well as Διός, Διί, Δία.

h. Σαρπηδών has Σαρπηδόνος Π 464, Σαρπήδοντος Μ 379.

i. κέλευθος and κύκλος are sometimes neuter in the plural.
So νευρή has νεῦρα Δ 122, πλευρή has πλευρά Δ 468.

j. Certain names of cities are found in both singular and
plural: Ἀθήνην η 80 but Ἀθήνας Β 546; Μυκήνη Δ 52,
Μυκήνας Β 569; Φηρῆ Ε 543, Φηράς Ι 151; Θήβης Δ 378,
Θήβας Ε 804.   Cf. Μάλειαν ι 80, Μαλειάων γ 287.   Instead
of the later plural Θεσπιαί, Πλαταιαί, Homer uses only the
singular: Θέσπειαν Β 498, Πλάταιαν Β 504.

ADJECTIVES.

§ 20. a. Some adjectives of three terminations are used
as if of two terminations, i.e. the masculine form is used also
for the feminine: ἰφθίμους ψυχάς Α 3, κλυτὸς Ἱπποδάμεια
Β 742, ἄγριον ἄτην Τ 88, ὀλοώτατος ὀδμή δ 442 where ὀλοω-
τάτη was metrically possible, ἠέρα πουλύν Ε 776, δεινὸς ἀήτη
Ο 626, ἀσπάσιος γῆ ψ 233, θερμὸς ἀυτμή μ 369, Πύλοιο ἠμα-
θόεντος Β 77, ὑλήεντι Ζακύνθῳ α 246 but ὑλήεσσα Ζάκυνθος
ι 24, ἁλὸς πολιοῖο Υ 229 but ἁλὸς πολιῆς Φ 59.

b. Compound adjectives, on the contrary, often have a
feminine form: ἀδμήτη, ἀθανάτη, ἀμφιελίσση, ἀριζήλη, ἀσβέ-
στη, εἰναλίη, ἐυξέστη, πολυμνήστη, πολυφόρβη.

c. The feminine of adjectives in -υς, ends in -ειᾰ (gen.
-ειης), -εᾰ (§ 5 g), or -εη (§ 5 b): βαθεῖα, βαθείης, — ὠκέα,
— βαθέης, βαθέην.

d. εὐρύς has acc. sing. masc. εὐρέα (in connection with
κόλπος and πόντος) as well as εὐρύν.

e. ἐύς good has gen. sing. ἐῆος, gen. plur. ἐάων.   But for
ἐῆος, the Alexandrian critic Zenodotus wrote ἐοῖο (possessive
pronoun) which is perhaps a better reading.

f. πολύς (πουλύς) has in the masculine and neuter both stems πολυ- (πουλυ-) and πολλο- (for πολυο-, § 19 *a*), with a nearly complete set of forms for each : πολλός and πολλόν, πολέος, πολέες, πολέων, πολέσσι, πολέσι, πολέεσσι, πολέας, with all the Attic forms except πολλοῦ.

g. πρέσβυς has feminine πρέσβα (as from πρέσβος), πρό-φρων has feminine πρόφρασσα, θοῦρος has feminine θουρίς.

PATRONYMICS.

§ 21. a. Suffixes which originally expressed connection or possession were used to form patronymic adjectives. The original force of these suffixes is occasionally preserved : (θεοὶ) Οὐρανίωνες A 570 is a mere adjective of connection like (θεοῖσιν) ἐπουρανίοισι Z 129 ; Homer does not recognize Οὐρανός as the ancestor of the gods. Ὀλυμπιάδες μοῦσαι B 491 is equivalent to μοῦσαι Ὀλύμπια δώματ᾽ ἔχουσαι B 484.

b. The importance which the Homeric Greeks attached to a son's connection with his father is not only indicated by the frequent use of patronymics as proper names (as Ἀτρεί-δης A 7, Μενοιτιάδη A 307, before the names *Agamemnon*, *Patroclus*, had been mentioned), but is shown also by K 68 f. where in great fear Agamemnon bids his brother to rouse the warriors πατρόθεν ἐκ γενεῆς ὀνομάζων ἄνδρα ἕκαστον | πάν-τας κυδαίνων, as in their great extremity before Syracuse Nicias, encouraging the Athenians, τῶν τριηράρχων ἕνα ἕκα-στον ἀνεκάλει, πατρόθεν τε ὀνομάζων καὶ φυλήν Thuc. VII 69. When a stranger was asked who he was, he gave his own name, that of his father and that of his country ; as a man's official name at Athens included that of his father and that of his deme (πατρόθεν καὶ τοῦ δήμου οὗ ἕκαστός ἐστι τὸ ὄνο-μα), *e.g.* Δημοσθένης Δημοσθένους Παιανιεύς *Demosthenes, son of Demosthenes, a Paeanian.*

A. c. The patronymic is formed from stems of the 1st declension by adding -δα- : Ἀργεάδην Π 417, Αὐγηιάδαο B 624, Ἱπποτάδης κ 2, or more frequently by adding -ιαδα- :

Λαερτιάδης Γ 200, Ἀγχισιάδης Ψ 296, in which the final α of the stem is lost.

d. This analogy, giving an ending in -ιάδης, is followed by stems in -ιο of the 2d declension: Μενοιτιάδης Ι 211. So also by stems of the 3d declension: Πηληιάδεω Α 1 (as well as Πηλεΐδης Σ 316, Πηλεΐωνα Α 197), Λαομεδοντιάδης Ο 527, Μηκιστηιάδης Ζ 28, even Ὀιλιάδης Π 330 from Ὀιλεύς. See *j* below.

e. The suffix -ιδα- is added to stems in ο, and the ο is lost as in *d* above: Κρονίδης, — also to stems in ευ, which lose their υ between two vowels (§ 5 *g*): Ἀτρεΐδης Α 7, — also to consonantal stems, as Ἀγαμεμνονίδης α 30. Δευκαλίδης (Δευκαλίδαο Μ 117) is formed as from Δεύκαλος, instead of from Δευκαλίων, and Ἀνθεμίδης Δ 488 as from Ἄνθεμος rather than from Ἀνθεμίων (Ἀνθεμίωνος υἱόν Δ 473). Possibly Δεύκαλος was a short form of Δευκαλίων, as a comrade of Achilles is called sometimes Ἀλκιμέδων (Π 197, Ρ 467), but sometimes Ἄλκιμος (Τ 392, Ω 474), and Λευκόλοφος Aristophanes *Frogs* 1513 is the same person as Λευκολοφίδης Plato *Protag.* 315 e. *Cf.* Σμινθεύς (Σμινθεῦ Α 39) for Σμινθοφθόρος and ἕκατος for ἑκατηβόλος (§ 4 *c*).

f. Patronymics from stems in -ευ, after the loss of the υ, do not in Homer suffer contraction of the ε of the stem with the ι of the suffix. The poet says Ἀτρεΐδης, Ἀτρεΐων, as tetrasyllables not trisyllables. The verse ictus never falls on the ει.

g. Female patronymics are formed by the suffix -ιδ- which loses δ before the nominative sign: Χρυσηΐδα (acc. of Χρυσηΐς) Α 182, Βρισηΐδα Α 184, Νηρηΐδες Σ 38, *daughters of Nereus*, Τρωιάδων Σ 122, *daughters of Tros*, Δαρδανίδων Σ 122, *daughters of Dardanus*, as the Trojans are called Δαρδανίωνες Η 414. Ἀχαιΐδες Β 235 corresponds to κοῦροι Ἀχαιῶν Α 473.

B. h. Patronymics are formed also by the suffix -ιον- ; Κρονίων Α 528 (with genitive Κρονίωνος or Κρονίονος, *cf.*

§ 22 k), Ἀτρείων, Πηλείων. In these last forms from nouns
in -ευς the ι is always short.

i. The corresponding female patronymic is found in Ἀδρη-
στίνη E 412, Ἀκρισιώνης Ξ 319 (gen. of Ἀκρισιώνη) daughter of Acrisius.

j. Ταλαϊονίδαο B 566 is irregular; it seems to be formed
by a cumulation of suffixes from Τάλαος, cf. Ἠελίου Ὑπεριονίδαο μ 176. So Λαομεδοντιάδης (Λαομεδοντιάδη Γ 250) is
formed from Λαομεδόντιος which itself appears as a patronymic (in the form Λαμεδόντιος) in a Boeotian inscription;
cf. Λαομεδόντιε παῖ Eur. Troad. 822. Αἴας Τελαμωνιάδης
Ψ 838 appears to have the same formation when compared
with Τελαμώνιος Αἴας Ψ 842.

Conversely, for Δευκαλίδης instead of Δευκαλιονίδης, see e
above.

k. Some adjectives in -ιος are used as patronymics, as Τελαμώνιος Αἴας B 528. Cf. Ποιάντιον υἱόν γ 190, Τελαμώνιε παῖ
Soph Aj. 134, Κρόνιε παῖ Pind. Ol. II 12. This formation
appears constantly on Thessalian and frequently on Boeotian
inscriptions. Cf. the nomina gentilicia of the Romans.

l. The patronymics in -δης are far more numerous than
those in -ιων; the former are found in Homer 708 times; the
latter, 148 times.

m. The patronymic is sometimes derived from the grandfather's name: Achilles is called Αἰακίδης B 860; Priam, Δαρδανίδης Γ 303; the two grandsons of Actor, Ἀκτορίωνε B 621.
Thus in later poetry, Heracles is called Alcides (Ἀλκείδης)
from Amphitryo's father Ἀλκαῖος or Ἀλκεύς.

COMPARISON OF ADJECTIVES.

§ **22. a.** Comparatives and superlatives end in -ιων, -ιστος
more frequently than in Attic: βραδύς, βάρδιστος, — βράσ-
σων probably from βραχύς, — γλυκύς, γλυκίων, — κακός, κα-
κίων as well as κακώτερος, — φίλος, φιλίων as well as φίλτε-
ρος, φίλτατος, — ὠκύς, ὤκιστος as well as ὠκύτατος.

b. Some comparatives and superlatives are formed from noun stems: βασιλεύτερος I 160, βασιλεύτατος I 69, θεώτεραι ν 111, κουροτέροισι Δ 316, κύντερον Θ 483, κύντατον Κ 503, — αἰσχίων, αἴσχιστος (αἶσχος), ἄλγιον, ἄλγιστος (ἄλγος), ἐλέγχιστος (ἔλεγχος), κέρδιον, κέρδιστος (κέρδος), κήδιστος (κῆδος), κύδιστος (κῦδος), μήκιστος (μῆκος), μακρότερος, μακρότατος, ῥίγιον, ῥίγιστος (ῥῖγος).

c. In some comparatives in -τερος, there is no thought of a greater or less degree but of a contrast, as ἀγροτεράων (ἡμιόνων) B 852 *of the field*, as opposed to the town; θηλύτεραι (γυναῖκες) Θ 520, *female*, as opposed to male; ὀρέστερος (δράκων) Χ 93, *of the mountain*, as opposed to the valley. *Cf.* ἡμέτερος, ὑμέτερος, δεξίτερος and ἀριστερός *right* and *left*.

d. From adverbs are formed: ἄγχιστος (ἆσσον, ἀσσοτέρω), ἀφάρτερος, παροίτερος, πρότερος, ὑπέρτατος.

e. ἀγαθός has comparatives ἀρείων (*cf.* ἄριστος), βέλτερον, λώιον, λωίτερον.

f. ἀνιηρός has a comparative ἀνιηρέστερον β 190.

g. νέος has a superlative νέαται I 153, νείατον B 824.

h. πολύς has a comparative πλείων or πλέων and in the plural also πλέες Λ 395, πλέας B 129.

i. φαεινός has a comparative φαεινότερος, a superlative φαάντατος ν 93 (for φαέντατος, *cf.* φάανθεν Α 200 for ἐφάενθεν).

j. ω is found where the Attic rule would require ο, in κακοξεινώτερος υ 376, λαρώτατος β 350, οἰζυρώτερον Ρ 446.

k. The ι of -ιων is regularly short as φιλίων τ 351 ; *cf.* the occasional ῑ of the patronymic in -ιων, § 21 *h*.

NUMERALS.

§ 23. a. ἑνί has a collateral form ἰῷ Ζ 422; *cf.* the feminine forms ἴᾰ Δ 437, ἰῆς Π 173, ἰῇ I 319, ἴᾰν ξ 435.

πρῶτος has a collateral form πρώτιστος, *cf.* πάμπρωτος Η 324.

Of the compound οὐδείς (οὐδ᾽ εἷς), besides οὐδέν, only οὐδενί is used (twice, X 459, λ 515); from μηδείς is found only μηδέν Σ 500.

b. δύω, δύο is indeclinable; it has the following collateral forms: δοιώ, δοιοί, δοιαί, δοιά, δοιοῖς, δοιούς.

δεύτερος has a superlative δεύτατος *last of all*, while δεύτερος has the comparative ending as the *latter of two*.

c. τρίτος has a collateral form τρίτατος, *cf.* μέσσατος with μέσσος.

d. τέσσαρες has a collateral form, the Aeolic πίσυρες, Ο 680. Its ordinal is τέτρατος, by metathesis (§ 13) for τέταρτος.

e. ὀκτώ has the ordinals ὀγδόατος, ὄγδοος. In η 261, ξ 287, ὄγδοον seems to have been substituted by error in all the Mss. for ὀγδόατον.

f. ἐννέα has the ordinal εἴνατος (ἔνγατος ?), ἔνατος.

g. δώδεκα has the collateral forms δυώδεκα and δυοκαίδεκα.

h. ἐνενήκοντα Β 602, has a collateral form ἐννήκοντα τ 174, with which may be compared ἐνήκοντα on an inscription of Drymaea in Phocis.

i. μυρία is not yet used as a numeral for 10,000, but only for a *countless* (*indefinitely large*) number.

PRONOUNS.

§ 24. I. Personal and Possessive Pronouns. a.

Sing. N.	ἐγώ, ἐγών.	σύ, τύνη (6 times).	
G.	ἐμεῖο, ἐμέο (Κ 124), ἐμεῦ, μεῦ, ἐμέθεν.	σεῖο, σέο, σεῦ, σέθεν, τεοῖο (Θ 37).	εἷο (Δ 400, χ 19), ἕο, εὗ, ἕθεν.
D.	ἐμοί, μοί.	σοί, τοί, τείν (5 times).	οἷ, ἑοῖ (Ν 495, δ 38).
A.	ἐμέ, μέ.	σέ.	ἕ, ἑέ (Υ 171, Ω 134), μίν.
Possessive.	ἐμός (ἐμή, ἐμόν).	σός, τεός.	ὅς, ἑός.
Dual N. A.	νῶι, νώ (as Acc., Ε 219, ο 475).	σφῶι, σφώ.	σφωέ.
G. D.	νῶιν (as gen. only Χ 88).	σφῶιν, σφῷν (δ 62).	σφωΐν.
Possessive.	νωίτερος.	σφωίτερος.	
Plur. N.	ἡμεῖς, ἄμμες.	ὑμεῖς, ὕμμες.	σφεῖων (4 times),
G.	ἡμείων (4 times), ἡμέων (9 times).	ὑμείων (4 times), ὑμέων (5 times).	σφέων (4 times), σφῶν (Μ 155, Τ 302).
D.	ἡμῖν, ἧμιν, ἄμμι(ν).	ὑμῖν, ὕμιν, ὕμμι.	σφίσι(ν), σφί(ν).
A.	ἡμέας, ἧμας (π 372), ἄμμε.	ὑμέας, ὕμμε.	σφέας, σφᾶς (Ε 567), σφέ (5 times).
Possessive.	ἡμέτερος, ἁμός (7 times).	ὑμέτερος, ὑμός.	σφέτερος, σφός.

b. The oblique cases of ἡμεῖς and ὑμεῖς are said to retract their accent to the first syllable when they are unemphatic or when the last vowel is short, as ἧμας π 372, ὕμεων Ο 494, ὕμιν α 373; but this rule is not observed constantly in the Mss., and editions vary.

c. The oblique cases of the 3d personal pronoun when enclitic are anaphoric, like αὐτοῦ κτλ. in Attic; when accented they have their original reflexive use, like Attic ἑαυτοῦ, ἐμαυτοῦ, σεαυτοῦ, κτλ., which compounds are posthomeric, and are not found even in Pindar.

μίν, σφωέ, σφωΐν, σφί, σφάς, and σφέ are always enclitic.

d. The Aeolic forms ἄμμες, ἄμμε, ὕμμες, ὕμμε generally might stand in the text for ἡμεῖς, ἡμᾶς κτλ. So, also, perhaps ἄμμος and ὕμμος should be written for the possessive forms ἀμός, ὑμός, to bring them into correspondence with the Aeolic personal pronouns.

e. For the relation of the form ἐμεῖο to ἐμέο, of σεῖο to σέο, κτλ., see § 5 *g*.

f. ἑός seems to stand for σεϜος *suus* (*cf*. the old Latin *sovos*). Its use is not confined strictly to the third person; it means simply *own* (*cf*. ἴδιος, only twice in Homer, from the same root), as οὔ τοι ἐγώ γε | ἧς (for ἐμῆς) γαίης δύναμαι γλυκερώτερον ἄλλο ἰδέσθαι ι 28 *I can see nothing sweeter than my own native land*, δώμασιν οἷσιν (for σοῖσιν) ἀνάσσοις α 402. It is with rare exceptions the possessive of οὗ in its reflexive, not in its anaphoric signification (see *c*). As this use of οὗ became less familiar to the Greeks, it is probable that other words and forms were occasionally substituted for forms of ἑός in the text of the poems.

II. Intensive Pronoun. **g.** αὐτός regularly retains its intensive force in the oblique cases, even when not connected with a noun expressed, often marking a contrast which it is difficult to render smoothly in the English idiom. *Cf*. § 1 *h fin*.

The presumption is always strongly in favor of the original meaning; but all shades of meaning are found from the strict intensive to the simple anaphoric use of the Attic dialect.

h. For αὔτως in the sense of ὡσαύτως, see *j* below. In this use it has a large variety of meanings, as (ἄφρονά τ) αὔτως Γ 220 *a mere (simpleton)* ; *without cause* A 520, *without a prize* A 133, *absolutely* B 138, *vainly* B 342, *without chariot* E 255. Most of these meanings are derived from *in the same way as before*, the connection determining the special sense of each passage.

III. Demonstrative Pronouns. **i.** The Attic article ὁ, ἡ, τό, generally retains its demonstrative force in Homer, but like the intensive pronoun in the oblique cases, appears occasionally in its Attic signification.

In their demonstrative use, ὁ, ἡ, οἱ, αἱ, are best written ὅ, ἥ, οἵ, αἵ.—τοί, ταί, τώς are used besides οἵ, αἵ, ὥς.

j. Thus the absence of the article does not mark a noun as indefinite; cf. ἄνδρα μοι ἔννεπε Μοῦσα a 1 with arma virumque cano. αὐτὴν ὁδόν θ 107 is equivalent to Attic τὴν αὐτὴν ὁδόν, and frequently αὔτως is equivalent to Attic ὡσαύτως (ὥς being the adverb of the article, see *k* below and § 38 *h*) while ὡς δ᾽ αὔτως Γ 339 is equivalent to Attic οὕτω δ᾽ ὡσαύτως.

k. The demonstrative article is often followed by a noun in apposition with it, as οἳ δ᾽ ἐχάρησαν Ἀχαιοί τε Τρῶές τε Γ 111, *but these rejoiced, both Achaeans and Trojans*, αὐτὰρ ὃ βοῦν ἱέρευσεν ἄναξ ἀνδρῶν Ἀγαμέμνων Β 402 *but he, Agamemnon, king of men, sacrificed an ox.*

l. The forms with initial τ often have a relative force, but refer only to a definite antecedent; this is a relic of paratactic construction (§ 3 *n*), as is particularly clear in ἀλλὰ τὰ μὲν πολίων ἐξεπράθομεν τὰ δέδασται Α 125 *but what we took as spoils from the cities, these have been divided.*

m. τοίσδεσσιν β 47, τοίσδεσι φ 93 belong to ὅδε. They are analogous to the Aeolic τῶνδεων of Alcaeus and to the τοῦννεουν (for τῶνεων, from ὅνε = ὅδε) of a Thessalian inscription.

n. κεῖνος is often found for ἐκεῖνος, as the adverb κεῖθι for ἐκεῖθι (only ρ 10), while ἐκεῖ is not Homeric.

IV. RELATIVE PRONOUNS. **o.** Besides the Attic forms, ὅ is used for ὅς, ὅου (better ὅο, § 17 *c*) for οὗ, ἔης Π 208 for ἧς (where for ἔης τὸ πρίν, ὅο πρόσθεν has been conjectured).

p. The forms ὅς and ὅ have also a demonstrative use, especially ὅς with οὐδέ, μηδέ, καί, and γάρ.

For the relative use of the article, see *l* above.

q. The neuter ὅ is frequently used as a conjunction, like quod. So also ὅτι and ὅ τε.

V. r. THE INDEFINITE AND INTERROGATIVE PRONOUNS have genitive singular τέο, τεῦ, dative τέῳ, genitive plural τέων, dative τέοισι, neuter plural of the indefinite ἄσσα only τ 218. The stem of τέο seems to be distinct in derivation from that of τίνος but identical in meaning.

s. In ὅ τις for ὅς τις (*cf.* ὅ for ὅς, ο above), the first stem often remains uninflected; ὅ τις, ὅτι or ὅττι, ὅτευ or ὅττεο, ὅτεῳ, ὅτινα, ὅτεων (ὧν τινων not being either Ionic or dactylic), ὁτέοισι, ὅτινας, neuter plural ἄσσα (ὅτινα X 450, but corrupt).

CONJUGATION.

§ 25. AUGMENT AND REDUPLICATION. a. The augment was for a time considered unessential: whether temporal or syllabic, it may be omitted in the Homeric poems; the accent is then thrown back as far as possible, as τεῦχε A 4, ὀλέκοντο A 10, ἀφίει A 25, κάθεμεν ι 72 (καθεῖμεν), ἄνεσαν Φ 537 (ἀνεῖσαν).

b. When the augment is omitted, monosyllabic forms with long vowel take the circumflex accent, as βῆ for ἔβη.

c. Iteratives generally have no augment, § 36 *a*.

d. Forms without the augment are less common in the speeches than in the narrative. In the narrative, the augmented preterits are to the unaugmented as 7 to 10, but in the speeches as 7 to 2.

e. The Mss. are frequently of less authority than the rhythm of the verse in determining whether a form should be augmented: *e.g.* at the close of the verse, ‒ ∪, ∪ ‒ ‒ (where the comma indicates the end of a word) was preferred to ‒ ∪ ∪, ‒ ‒; hence ἄλγε᾽ ἔθηκεν A 2, not ἄλγεα θῆκεν (§ 40 *k*); τεύχε᾽ ἔκειτο Γ 327, not τεύχεα κεῖτο. To write ἑλώρι᾽ ἔτευχε κύνεσσιν A 4, or δὲ τελείετο βουλή A 5, would create the forbidden caesura between the short syllables of the fourth foot (§ 40 *m*). For the same reason the augment is omitted also when it would interfere with the Bucolic diaeresis (§ 40 *h*), as μία γείνατο μήτηρ Γ 238.

f. After the augment, initial λ, μ, or σ is sometimes doubled (in many instances as the assimilation of an original F or σ) as well as initial ρ: ἐλλιτάνευσα κ 481, ἔλλαβε α 298, ἔμμαθες σ 362, ἔσσευε Λ 147 (see § 41 *j a*).

g. Sometimes initial ρ is not doubled, as ἐράπτομεν π 379, ἔρεξα δ 352, ἔρεζε Β 400; *cf.* ἐρρύσατο καὶ ἐσάωσεν Ο 290 with ἐρύσατο καὶ ἐσάωσεν χ 372. See § 12 *c*.

h. Stems which originally began with a consonant may take the syllabic augment or reduplication, as ἔειπον, ἔηκε, ἐάγη, ἐάλην, ἐέλπετο, — ἔοικα, ἔολπα, ἔοργε, ἐέλμεθα Ω 662. Thus εἶδον is for ἐ-Fιδ-ον, εἶρπον is for ἐ-σερπ-ον. In ἔρχαται κ 283, this reduplication seems to be lost, *cf.* ἐέρχατο κ 241; so δέχαται Μ 147, ἔσσαι ω 250. In ἤικτο, as δ 796, and ἠεί-δης Χ 280, the η is the augment lengthened by the following F (Fικ- and Fιδ-). See § 41 *d*.

i. In the usual texts, many of these verbs have the temporal augment; this probably was not so spoken in the original form of the poems, but is a conformation to later usage. δ' ἔανασσε is the rational, more original form for the Ms. reading δ' ἤνασσε γ 304, ἄνδανε for ἤνδανε Α 24, ἐάνδανε for ἐήνδανε γ 143, ἔαξε for ἦξε Ψ 392, ἐάλω for ἥλω χ 230. See § 4 *h*.

j. The second aorist active and middle, of verbs whose stem begins with a consonant, is often found with a reduplicated stem, as ἐκέκλετο, λελάχωσι, ἀμπεπαλών, ἐπέφραδε, πεπι-θοίμην, ἔτετμε, τετύκοντο.

k. The so-called *Attic reduplication* is more common in Homer than in Attic, and its use extends to the second aorist where the augment also may be used (*cf.* Attic ἤγαγον), as ἤραρε, ἤκαχε, ἄλαλκε, and the peculiar forms ἐρύκακε Λ 352 from ἐρύκω, ἠνίπαπε Β 245 from ἐνίπτω in which the final consonant of the theme is reduplicated with α as a connective (ἐνένιπε, as σ 321, is found more frequently).

l. In the perfect, the vowel after the Attic reduplication is not always lengthened, as ἀλάλημαι, while it is never lengthened in the aorist (§ 31 *f*).

m. A reduplicated future is foı ıed from the stem of some of these reduplicated aorists, as κεκαδήσει φ 153 from the stem of κεκάδοντο Δ 497, πεπιθήσω Χ 223, πεφιδήσεται Ω 158.

n. The reduplication of ῥερυπωμένα ζ 59, ἐκτῆσθαι Ι 402, is not according to Attic usage. δειδέχαται (from δείκνυμι), δείδοικα, and δείδια have irregular reduplication; probably the last two are to be explained as for δεδϝοικα, δεδϝια (§ 41 *l* β).

o. ἔμμορε (from μείρομαι) and ἔσσυμαι (from σεύω) double the initial consonant and prefix ε as if they began with two consonants (§ 41 *j* a).

§ 26. Endings.

a. The singular endings, -μι, -σθα, -σι, occur more frequently than in Attic; especially -μι and -σι in the subjunctive, as ἴδωμι, ἀγάγωμι, ἐθέλῃσι, βάλῃσι. These endings are rare in the subjunctive of the contracted μι-forms, as δῶσι Α 129, φθῆσιν Ψ 805, ᾖσι Ο 359.

b. -σθα is used three times in the optative, as βάλοισθα Ο 571; 29 times in the subjunctive, in 12 verbs, as εἴπῃσθα Τ 250, πάθῃσθα Ω 551; 8 times in the present indicative, in five verbs, as φῇσθα Φ 186.

c. In three verbs -τον is used for -την as the ending of the third person dual imperfect: ἐτεύχετον Ν 346, διώκετον Κ 364, λαφύσσετον Σ 583. -την would have made an *amphimacer* — ◡ —. See § 41 a.

d. The third plural of the perfect active ends in ᾶσι (for -αντι); ᾶσι is found only in πεφύκᾶσι η 114, λελόγκᾶσι λ 304.

e. In the pluperfect, the older endings -εα κτλ. are preserved, as ᾔδεα Ξ 71, πεποίθεα δ 434, ἠείδης Χ 280. The third singular ends in -εε(ν) or -ειν, as βεβήκειν Α 221, ᾔδεε Β 409.

f. The second and third persons singular of the first aorist optative active end in -ειας, -ειε(ν), as μείνειας, καλέσειεν. The second person in -αις occurs very rarely; the third per-

son in -αι is more common, as γηθῆσαι Α 255, ἀείραι Η 130.
The third plural with but two exceptions (κήαιεν, κτερίσαιεν
Ω 38) ends in -ειαν, as τίσειαν Α 42, ἀκούσειαν Β 282.

g. The third plural optative active of μι-verbs ends in -ιεν
(except σταίησαν Ρ 733), as εἶεν, δαμεῖεν, δοῖεν.

h. The second singular imperative ending -θι is retained
in some presents, as ἵληθι γ 380, δίδωθι γ 380, ὄμνυθι Ψ 585;
and in some perfects, as τέθναθι Χ 365, τέτλαθι Α 586.

i. The third plural imperative ends in -των, -σθων (never
-τωσαν, -σθωσαν), as ἔστων Α 338, φευγόντων Ι 47, λεξά-
σθων Ι 67.

j. *a.* Active infinitives (except in the first aorist) frequently end in -μεναι, which is sometimes shortened after a
short vowel to -μεν, as ἔμμεναι, ἔμμεν, ἐλθέμεν(αι), τεθνά-
μεν(αι).

β. The shortening of -μεναι to -μεν occurs generally before
a vowel, where it may be called elision.

γ. The ending -ναι is found only after a long vowel, as
δοῦναι, διδοῦναι Ω 425.

k. The ending in -εμεν is clearly preferred to that in -ειν
before the Bucolic diaeresis (§ 40 *h*); even before the diaeresis at the end of the first foot of the verse, the ending -εμεν
could stand ten times as often as the ending -ειν is required.

l. The second aorist active infinitive in 12 verbs, and the
future active infinitive in 9 verbs, have the anomalous ending -εειν, which probably stands for -εμεν or -εεν, which may
be restored.

m. Aorist passive infinitives end in -μεναι or -ναι, as δαμή-
μεναι Υ 266, δαμῆναι Φ 578; μιχθήμεναι Λ 438, μιγήμεναι
Ζ 161, μιγῆναι λ 306.

n. The perfect participle has the inflection of the present
in κεκλήγοντες Μ 125. See § 31 *d, e.*

o. Some second perfect participles retain in the oblique
cases the ω of the nominative, as τεθνηῶτος α 289, βεβαῶτα
ε 130.

p. The second singular of the middle generally remains uncontracted (§ 6), as ὀδύρεαι, ἴδηαι Γ 130, βάλλεο Α 297, ὠδύσαο α 62, ἐμάρναο χ 228. Contracted forms are used occasionally, as μετατρέπῃ Α 160, γνώσῃ Β 365, κεκλήσῃ Γ 138; once in the imperfect, ἐκρέμω Ο 18.

q. In the perfect middle, -σαι regularly loses its σ; but μέμνησαι Ψ 648 is found as well as μέμνηαι Φ 442, μέμνῃ Ο 18 (for μέμνεσαι, as if from μέμνομαι).

-σο retains its σ only in the imperative, as ἕσσο, ἵστασο.

r. The first person dual of the middle once ends in -μεθον, περιδώμεθον Ψ 485 (cf. λελείμμεθον Soph. *El.* 950, ὁρμώμεθον *Phil.* 1079) but the metre would admit περιδώμεθα with hiatus at the Bucolic diaeresis (§ 9 b).

s. The first plural middle often ends in -μεσθα (which is found also in the tragic poets), as ἱκόμεσθα γ 61.

t. The third plural of the perfect and pluperfect indicative middle often, and of the optative middle always, ends in -αται, -ατο for -νται, -ντο, as δεδαίαται α 23, πεφοβήατο Φ 206, γενοίατο α 266. Before these endings, smooth labial and palatal mutes are aspirated, as ὀρωρέχαται Π 834 from ὀρέγω, τετράφατο Κ 189 from τρέπω.

Attic prose writers use these endings sporadically in the perfect and pluperfect; but the tragic poets use this ending only in the optative (as γνωσοίατο Soph. *O. T.* 1274, cf. *Ajax* 842, *El.* 211; δεξαίατο *O. C.* 44, cf. 945; cf. also θείατο Aesch. *Suppl.* 665).

u. δ seems to be inserted in the forms ἀκηχέδαται Ρ 637 (ἀκαχίζω), ἐληλέδατο η 86 (ἐλαύνω), ἐρράδαται υ 354 (ῥαίνομαι). These forms probably came from collateral verb-stems which contained δ, cf. ῥάσσατε υ 150 (ῥαίνομαι for ῥαδνjω).

For ἐληλέδατο, Dindorf and Nauck read the less anomalous form ἐληλέατο, La Roche reads ἐληλάδατο.

v. The third plural indicative of the aorist passive generally ends in -εν instead of -ησαν (46 forms in -εν to 15 in

-ησαν), as ἤγερθεν Α 57, φάανθεν Α 200, τράφεν Α 251, διέτμαγεν Α 531.

w. Similarly, ν is used for the later -σαν in the imperfect
and second aorist of μι-verbs, as ξύνιεν Α 273, ἔστἄν, στἄν,
ἔβαν, ἔφυν ε 481, ἔτλαν Φ 608.

For the optative ending of μι-verbs, in -ιεν not -ιησαν, see
g above.

§ 27. Subjunctive Mode.

a. The variable vowel ("con-
necting vowel") of the subjunctive is generally short in the
first aorist, second aorist of μι-forms, second aorist passive,
second perfect of primitive formation, as βήσομεν, ἀγείρομεν,
ἴομεν, θείομεν, τραπείομεν, δαμείετε, εἴδομεν, πεποίθομεν.

This short vowel is found before the endings -μεν, -τον, -τε,
and in middle forms.

b. A few forms of the first aorist have a long vowel following the analogy of the present, as δηλήσηται Γ 107.

c. There are no certain examples of the short mode-vowel
in the present of verbs in -ω. (For βούλεται ἀντιάσας Α 67,
βούλητ᾽ ἀντιάσας may be substituted, *etc.*)

Rem. The forms of the first aorist subjunctive are easily con-
fused with those of the future, with which they are identical in
appearance.

§ 28. Optative Mode.

a. For the optative endings, see
§ 26 *b, f, g, t*.

b. After ι or υ, the optative sign disappears: δαινῦτο Ω
665, δύη σ 348, ἐκδῦμεν Π 99, λελῦντο σ 238, φθίμην κ 51,
φθῖτο λ 330, δαινύατο σ 248.

c. ἄλφοιεν is contracted to ἄλφοιν υ 383.

§ 29. Contract Verbs.

I. a. Verbs in -αω exhibit un-
changed, assimilated, and contracted forms; the poet's choice
between contracted and uncontracted forms seems to have
been determined largely by the rhythm. The vowels are
regularly contracted when the second is in a short syllable.

b. Uncontracted forms without assimilation occur rarely (in only 21 verbs), as ἀναμαιμάει Υ 490 (with long *a* as in διψάων λ 584, πεινάων Γ 25), ναιετάουσι ζ 153, ἀοιδιάει κ 227, οὔταε χ 356 (οὖτα, Δ 525 and often, is a second aorist, see § 35), κραδάων Η 213.

σάω imperfect, Φ 238, and imperative, ν 230, is a μι-form, as if from σάωμι.

c. The vowels of the uncontracted forms are generally assimilated, *a* prevailing over a following ε or η but being assimilated to ο, ω, or ου. These forms are intermediate between the original and the contracted stage, as ὁρόωσιν θ 173 (ὁράουσιν, ὁρῶσιν), ἡβώοντες Ω 604, ἐλάαν γ 484 (ἐλα-εν, ἐλᾶν). ἀλόω ε 377 seems to be for ἀλαε-ο contracted to ἀλᾱ-ο (*cf. h* below), with assimilation of vowels ἀλω-ο, and by transposition of quantity ἀλό-ω.

d. One of the vowels is usually lengthened in the text of the Mss., as ὁρόωντες η 145. Sometimes this appears to be a conformation to Attic usage (§ 4 *h*).

e. Dual forms follow the analogy of Homeric verbs in -μι, as ἀπειλήτην λ 313, προσαυδήτην Λ 136. *Cf. j* below, and ὄρηαι ξ 343 as from ὄρημι.

f. A few verbs in -αω have collateral forms in -εω, as ἤντεον Η 423.

II. g. Verbs in -εω generally remain uncontracted; except εε, which is generally contracted in the Mss., but often the uncontracted forms are metrically possible. εο is very rarely contracted except in the participle ending -ευμενος (where contraction occurs to prevent a too frequent recurrence of short syllables, § 41 *g*). εω is never contracted but is often pronounced as one syllable by synizesis (§ 7).

h. Sometimes the variable vowel ε is contracted with ε of the stem instead of with the termination, as αἰδεῖο Ω 503 (αἰδεσ-ε-σο), μυθεῖαι θ 180, σπεῖο Κ 285. σπεῖο seems to be formed on the analogy of αἰδεῖο. One of these vowels is sometimes dropped, as ἀποαίρεο Α 275, ἔκλεο Ω 202, μυθέαι β 202, πωλέαι δ 811. The accentuation of these last three forms is uncertain.

i. The older form of these verbs, in -ειω, is sometimes preserved, as ἐτελείετο Α 5, νεικείῃσι Α 579. See § 5 *f.*

j. Some verbs in -αω and -εω have a present infinitive in -ημεναι, like μι-verbs, as ἀρήμεναι χ 322, καλήμεναι Κ 125, ποθήμεναι μ 110, φιλήμεναι Χ 265. See § 34 *b.*

φορέω forms φορέειν Δ 144, φορήμεναι Ο 310, φορῆναι Β 107.

III. k. Verbs in -οω are generally contracted. Sometimes they have forms with the double ο sound, like verbs in -αω, as ἀρόωσιν ι 108 (ἀροουσιν, ἀροῦσιν), ὑπνώοντας ε 48, ἐστρατόωντο Γ 187 (which might be written ἐστρατόοντο), δηιόῳεν δ 226 (δηιόοιεν?).

TENSES.

§ 30. Future and First Aorist, Active and Middle.
a. Pure verbs which do not lengthen the stem-vowel in the formation of the tenses, often have double σ in the future and first aorist, active and middle, as αἰδέσσομαι ξ 388, κάλεσσα Ω 106.

b. In the future the σ of the before-mentioned verbs often disappears, as καλέουσα Γ 383, ἀντιόων α 25, κορέει Θ 379 (for κορέσει, from κορέννυμι), δαμάᾳ Χ 271, κρεμόω Η 83, *cf.* κομιῶ ο 546; ὀλέσσει β 49, ὀλέσω ν 399, ὀλεῖται Β 325.

c. Stems in δ often show double σ in the aorist.

d. Most of these forms with σσ may be explained as original or assimilated, as νείκεσσε from the theme νεικεσ (*cf.* νεῖκος), κομίσσατο for κομιδ-σατο (*cf.* κομιδή). Thus the stem-vowel of these verbs was not final originally, and hence is not lengthened in the future and aorist.

e. The asigmatic future of liquid verbs is inflected like the present of verbs in -εω, as βαλέει κ 290, ὀλέεσθαι Ο 700. See § 29 II.

f. Some stems in λ and ρ retain the σ of the future and aorist (as some do in Attic), as ἄρσας (ἀραρίσκω) α 280, ἔλσαι Α 409, θερσόμενος τ 507, κύρσας Γ 23, διαφθέρσει Ν 625, ἐκέλσαμεν ι 546, ὦρσε Α 10. For ὀφέλλειεν β 334, see § 12 e.

g. The so-called Doric future with tense-sign σε, is found in ἐσσεῖται Β 393, πεσέονται Λ 824. This is an archaism, not a Dorism.

h. Some verbs have a future without tense-sign, as δήεις ζ 291 *shalt find*, εἶμι, κείω τ 340 *shall lie* (κακκείοντες α 424 *to lie down*), ἔδομαι, πίομαι, ἀνύω, ἐρύω, βέομαι Ο 194 (βείομαι Χ 431). Some of these verbs are old presents which acquired a future signification; εἶμι is not always future in Homer, *cf.* Β 87.

i. Some verbs form the first aorist active and middle without σ, as ἤνεικαν δ 784 (Attic ἤνεγκα), ἔχευεν β 395 and ἔχεεν Ζ 419 (from ἔχεα for ἔχευα), ἔσσευα Ε 208, ἠλεύατο Χ 274 and ἀλέασθε δ 774, ἔκηα Α 40, subjv. κήομεν Η 377 (from καίω).

j. The first aorist often has the variable vowel of the second aorist °/ₑ, as ἷξον γ 5, δύσετο β 388. So in the imperative, as βήσεο Ε 109, ὄρσεο Γ 250, ἄξετε Γ 105, οἴσετε Γ 103, ὄψεσθε Ω 704; infinitive, οἰσέμεναι Γ 120; participle, δυσομένοιο α 24 and probably ἐπιβησόμενον Π 343.

k. Verbs in -ζω often have themes in γ and thus futures and first aorists in -ξω and -ξα, as ἐξαλαπάξαι Α 129, μερμήριξε β 93, πτολεμίξομεν Β 328.

l. The future optative is not found in Homer.

31. PERFECT. a. The so-called first perfect in -κα is formed only from 20 vowel-stems. It is almost as rare as the first aorist in -κα (ἔδωκα, ἔηκα, ἔθηκα). Forms without κ are derived even from vowel-stems, especially participial forms, as κέκμηκας Ζ 262, but κεκμηὼς Ψ 232; πεφύκασι η 114 but πεφύασιν η 128 ἐμπεφυῖα Α 513; τέθνηκεν α 196, τεθνηκυῖαν δ 734, but τεθνηότα Ρ 402.

b. The final mute of the stem is not aspirated.

c. The endings are affixed immediately to the reduplicated verb-stem in βεβάασι, γεγάασι, δείδιθι, δείδιμεν, ἐδείδισαν, ἐγρή-

γορθε, εἴκτον, εἰλήλουθμεν, ἴδμεν, κεκμηώς, μέματον, πέποσθε,
ἐπέπιθμεν, ἔστατε, τετλαίη, τέτλαθι, τέθνασαν.

d. ἤνωγον (as ζ 216), μέμηκον (as ι 439), γέγωνε (as θ 305)
are inflected as imperfects; cf. ἐρρίγῃσι Γ 353, ὀλώλῃ Δ 164,
which have the force of present subjunctives.

e. ἀλαλήμενος, ἀλάλησθαι, ἀκαχήμενος, ἀκάχησθαι, ἐσσύμενος are accented irregularly as presents. See § 26 n.

f. The second perfect often has a long vowel in the stem
where the second aorist has a short vowel, as ἀρήρῃ ε 361,
ἀράρῃ Π 212; ὄρωρε Η 374, ὤρορε Β 146.

g. In the feminine participle the short form of the stem
appears, as ἀρηρώς κ 553 but ἀραρυῖα ζ 267, τεθηλώς μ 103
but τεθαλυῖα ζ 293; hence εἰκυῖα not εἰκυῖα Γ 386, etc.

VOICES.

§ 32. MIDDLE. a. The active and middle forms ὁρᾶν
(about 40 times) and ὁρᾶσθαι (about 20 times), ἰδεῖν (more
than 200 times) and ἰδέσθαι (90 times), are used often without appreciable difference of meaning; cf. ἔφατο β 267, ἔφη
β 377.

b. The first aorist middle is sometimes used without difference of meaning from the second aorist active, as ἐβήσετο
η 135, ἔβη α 427; ἐδύσετο Γ 328, ἔδυ Γ 36; κιχήσατο Δ 385,
ἔκιχεν γ 169.

c. The future middle is sometimes used as passive, as διαρραίσεσθαι Ω 355, πέρσεται Ω 729, τελέεσθαι Β 36. Cf. e.

d. The aorist middle is sometimes used with no distinction of meaning from the passive, as κοιμήσαντο Α 476, κοι-
μήθημεν ι 559; χολωσαμένη Γ 413, χολωθείς Α 9; ἐδυνήσατο
Ξ 33, δυνάσθη ε 319; χήρατο Ξ 270, χάρη Γ 76 (cf. κεχαροίατο Α 256); ἀπενάσσατο Β 629, νάσθη Ξ 119; ἀγέροντο Β 94,
ἤγερθεν Α 57; λύμην Φ 80, λύθεν Σ 31; ἀμφέχυτο Β 41, ἀμφε-
χύθη δ 716; cf. κτάσθαι Ο 558 *be slain*, κταμένοιο Γ 375;
and ἐλελίχθησαν Ε 497 *they rallied*, θωρηχθῆναι Α 226 *arm
himself*, ἰθυνθήτην Π 475.

e. Homer has only ἀρνήσασθαι, ἠρασάμην, ἤσατο, ὀρέξατο, never the corresponding passive forms.

33. PASSIVE.   **a.** For the ending of the aorist passive infinitive, see § 26 *m*.

b. For the ending of the third plural indicative, see § 26 *v*.

c. The second aorist subjunctive passive usually remains uncontracted, and follows the rule of μι-verbs (§ 34 *d*).

d. In the second aorist subjunctive, the passive suffix is often long (and the mode-vowel short in the dual and in the first or second person plural, § 27 *a*), as δαείω ι 280 (from stem δα-, *cf.* δαῆναι), δαμήῃς Γ 436 (δάμνημι), σαπήῃ Τ 27 (σήπω), δαμήετε Η 72, τραπείομεν Γ 441 (τέρπω, § 13), but μιγέωσιν Β 475 (μίσγω).

e. Homer has only two futures from passive stems, δαήσεαι γ 187, μιγήσεσθαι Κ 365.

f. Some verbs have both first and second aorists passive, as ἐβλάφθησαν Ψ 387, ἔβλαβεν Ψ 461; ἐμίχθη Ε 134, ἐμίγην Γ 445; πῆχθεν Θ 298, πάγεν Λ 572; ἐτέρφθητε ρ 174, τάρφθη φ 57, ἐτάρπησαν Ω 633, τραπείομεν Γ 441, with τεταρπώμεσθα Ψ 10 in the same sense.

VERBS IN –MI.

34. **a.** Some verbs in -μι have forms in the present and imperfect indicative which follow the analogy of contract verbs: τιθεῖ α 192, διδοῖ δ 237, διδοῦσι α 313, ἱεῖσι Γ 152, ἐδίδου λ 289, ἐτίθει β 390 ; so δαμνᾷ λ 221, πίτνα Φ 7, ἐκίρνα η 182, ὤρννε φ 100.

b. Verbs in -μι sometimes retain the long vowel of the stem where it is short in Attic, as τιθήμεναι Ψ 83 (for τιθέναι), *cf.* φιλήμεναι Χ 265; τιθήμενον Κ 34 (for τιθέμενον). διδώσομεν ν 358 (δώσομεν) and διδοῦναι Ω 425 are irregular.

c. For the ending -ν for -σαν, see § 26 *w*.

d. The second aorist subjunctive active generally remains uncontracted.   The stem vowel often appears in its long

form with short mode vowel in the dual and in the first and
second plural (*cf.* §§ 27 *a*, 33 *d*), as θείω *a* 89 (better θήω),
γνώω ξ 118, στήῃς P 30, δώῃσιν A 324, παρστήετον σ 183,
θείομεν A 143 (better θήομεν), γνώωσι A 302, ἐρείομεν A 62
(better ἐρήομεν, as from an ἔρημι).

e. ἵημι *send* has the following not-Attic forms: ἱεῖσι (ἱᾶσι),
ἱῆσι (ἱῇ) ἵεν (ἵεσαν), ἱέμεναι (ἱέναι), ἀνέσει (ἀνήσει), ἔηκα
(ἧκα), κάθεμεν (καθεῖμεν), ἔσαν, εἷσαν (ἧκαν), μεθείω (μεθῶ),
ἧσι, ἀφέῃ, ἀνήῃ (ἀνῇ), μεθέμεν (μεθεῖναι), ἔντο (εἷντο).

f. *a.* εἶμι *go* or *shall go* is aoristic except in the present
indicative. It has the following not-Attic forms: εἶσθα
(thrice for εἶ), ἤια, ἀνήιον (ᾖα), ἤιε, ᾖε, ἴε(ν) (ᾔει), ἴτην
(ᾔτην), ᾔομεν, ἴμεν (ᾖμεν), ἤισαν, ἴσαν, ἤιον (ᾖσαν), ἤισθα
(ἴῃς), ἴησιν (ἴῃ), ἴομεν, ἴομεν (ἴωμεν), ἰείη (ἴοι), ἴμεν(αι)
(ἰέναι), fut. εἴσομαι, aor. εἴσατο, ἐείσατο.

β. Perhaps ἤιμεν, ἤισαν should be read for ᾖομεν, ᾖον.

g. *a.* εἰμί *am* has the following not-Attic forms: ἐσσί,
εἶς (also enclitic, somewhat less frequent than ἐσσί, which
consists of the original stem ἐσ- and the original ending of
the second person -σι, which generally can be substituted for
it) (εἶ), εἰμέν (ἐσμέν), ἔασι (εἰσί), ἦα, ἔα, ἔον (ἦν), ἔησθα
(ἦσθα), ἦεν, ἔην, ἤην (ἦν), ἔσαν (ἦσαν), ἔω, μετείω (ὦ), ἔῃς,
ἦσιν (ᾖς), ἔωσι (ὦσι), ἔοις (εἴης), ἔοι (εἴη), ἔσσο, a form of
the middle voice, as also Sappho 1 28, (ἴσθι), ἔμμεν(αι), by
assimilation for ἐσ-μεναι, ἔμεν(αι) (εἶναι), ἐών, ἐοῦσα κτλ. (ὤν,
οὖσα κτλ.), ἔσσεται, ἐσσεῖται (twice, for ἔσται). Iterative
ἔσκον, ἔσκε.

β. ἔην, ἤην (ἦν), probably should be written ἔεν, ἦεν.

γ. Forms without the root-vowel ε (remnant of ἐσ-) are
very rare, as ἦσιν T 202, ὦσι Ξ 274, ω 491, οὔσης τ 489, ὄν-
τας η 94; ἦν is more common but often can be written ἔεν.

h. φημί *say* has the following not-Attic forms: φῆσθα
(φῆς), ἔφαν, φάν (ἔφασαν), φήῃ, φῆσιν (φῇ). Middle forms
are common, but not in the present indicative: ἐφάμην, ἔφατο,
ἔφαντο, imperative φάο, φάσθω, infinitive φάσθαι, participle

φάμενος. Iterative ἔφασκον κτλ. πεφασμένον Ξ 127 may come from φαίνω.

i. κεῖμαι *lie* has the following not-Attic forms: κείαται, κέαται, κέονται (κεῖνται), κείατο, κέατο (ἔκειντο), κῆται (from κέεται for κέηται). Iterative κέσκετο. For the future κείω, κείων, κείοντες, see § 30 *h*.

j. *a.* ἧμαι *sit* has εἵαται, ἕαται (ἧνται), εἵατο, ἕατο (ἧντο Γ 153).

β. ἥαται and ἥατο are more rational forms than εἵαται and εἵατο, which are found in the Mss.

k. οἶδα *know* has the following not-Attic forms: οἶδας (only *a* 337, for οἶσθα), ἴδμεν (ἴσμεν), ἤδεα (ᾔδη), ᾐείδης (see § 41 *d*, for ᾔδησθα), ᾐείδει, ᾔδεε (ᾔδει), ἴσαν (ᾖσαν), ἴδμεν(αι) (εἰδέναι), ἰδυῖα (εἰδυῖα). Future εἰδήσω as well as εἴσομαι.

l. χρή in Homer seems to be a noun. See § 3 *k*.

§ 35. Second Aorists without Variable Vowel.

Many second aorists, active and middle, are found without variable vowel, following the analogy of verbs in -μι, as ἔκτα *a* 300, ἔκτατο Ο 437 (from κτείνω, stem κτεν-, κτα-); ἆλσο Π 754, ἆλτο Λ 532 (ἅλλομαι); ἄμεναι Φ 70 (ἄω); γέντο Θ 43; ἐγήρα Η 148, γηράς Ρ 197 (γηράω); ἔγνω Λ 199; δέκτο Β 420 (δέχομαι); βλῆτο Δ 518 (βάλλω); κλῦθι β 262, κλῦτε Β 56 (κλύω); ἔμικτο *a* 433; οὖτα Ζ 64, οὐτάμεναι ι 301; πλῆτο Σ 50; ἐπέπλως γ 15 (πλώω); ἔσσυτο Β 809 (σεύω); ἔφθιτο Σ 100, φθίσθαι β 183, φθίμενος Θ 359 (φθίνω).

ITERATIVE FORMS.

§ 36. a. Iterative forms of the imperfect and aorist indicate the repetition of a state or action. The augment is generally omitted. These forms are characterized by the suffix -σκ and have the inflection of the imperfect of verbs in -ω. They are confined to the Ionic dialect. The iterative idea is frequently waning and occasionally is lost.

b. Verbs in -ω add the endings -σκον or -σκομην to the

ε-form of the stem of the present or second aorist, as ἔχεσκον, ἔλεσκε, εἴπεσκε, ἴδεσκε.

c. κρύπτασκε Θ 272 probably should be κρύπτεσκε. ῥίπτασκε θ 374 probably should be ῥίψασκε, although both may be considered as formed according to mistaken analogy.

d. Iteratives from the first aorist are peculiar to Homer, ἐλάσασκε (ἐλαύνω), μνησάσκετο (μιμνήσκω), θρέξασκον (τρέχω).

e. The suffix is sometimes added without variable vowel to themes which end in a vowel, as ἔασκες Τ 295, ὤθεσκε λ 596, φάνεσκε λ 587 (the only example of a passive).

f. Verbs in -μι add the endings -σκον or -σκομην directly to the theme: ἔφασκον, δόσκον, δύσκεν, κέσκετο (κεῖμαι), ἔσκον (for ἐσ-σκον, εἰμί).

PREPOSITIONS.

§ 37. a. Prepositions often retain their original adverbial force (as ἐν δέ *but therein*, παρὰ δέ *and beside him*). They may be placed after the verbs or nouns with which they are connected. See § 3 *d*.

b. *a.* The preposition is often separated from the verb which it modifies, as πὰρ δὲ Κεφαλλήνων ἀμφὶ στίχες οὐκ ἀλαπαδναί | ἔστασαν Δ 330 f., where πάρ modifies ἔστασαν. In ἐν δὲ πυρὶ πρήσαντες Η 429, ἐν is to be construed adverbially, while πυρί is dative of means.

β. Sometimes the preposition, like other adverbs of place, governs a genitive where in its prepositional use it would be followed by another case, as τὸν μοχλὸν ὑπὸ σποδοῦ ἤλασα ι 375 *I drave the bar under the ashes*, where ὑπὸ σποδόν would be more regular.

γ. Similarly other words which were separate in the Homeric age were welded together in later time: οὐ γὰρ ἔτι became οὐκέτι γάρ, διὰ δ' ἀμπερές Λ 377 became διαμπερὲς δέ. So in old English *to us ward* was used where the later idiom requires *toward us; be thou ware* for *beware!*

c. ANASTROPHE. *a.* Disyllabic prepositions, when they immediately follow the word with which they are construed, take the accent upon the penult, except ἀμφί, ἀντί, ἀνά, διά. ἄνα Z 331 stands for ἀνάστηθι. ἔνι is used for ἔνεισι or ἔνεστι, ἔπι for ἔπεστι, μέτα for μέτεστι. ἄπο is used for ἄποθεν *far from.* πέρι is used for περισσῶς *exceedingly.*

β. Elided prepositions suffer anastrophe only when they as adverbs modify a verb to be supplied, as ἔπ' Γ 45 for ἔπεστι,—or by way of exception, in order to avoid ambiguity, as ἔφ' A 350, to show that the preposition is to be connected with the preceding word; so πάρ' Σ 191, κάτ' ρ 246.

γ. This so-called retraction of the accent to the first syllable is only a conservation of its original position, from which it was moved when the adverb lost something of its independence by its close connection with a verb or noun.

d. *a.* ἐν has the parallel forms εἰν, εἰνί, ἐνί. εἰν stands only in the part of the foot which receives the ictus, and its use is nearly confined to certain phrases, as εἰν ἀγορῇ, εἰν 'Αίδαο δόμοισιν. εἰνί is used but half a dozen times and only in the second foot.

β. The poet uses both ἐς and εἰς, κατά and καταί (in καταιβαταί ν 110), παρά and παραί, πρός, προτί, and ποτί, ὑπό and ὑπαί, ὑπέρ and ὑπείρ.

γ. The forms in -αι seem to be old locatives, *cf.* χαμαί (*humi*).

e. ἐξ receives an accent when, following its noun, it stands at the end of the verse, as θεῶν ἔξ ρ 518, or is in danger of a wrong construction, as θεῶν ἔξ ἔμμορε τιμῆς ε 335 *from the gods she has received a share of honor.*

f. ἀμφί, ἀνά, and μετά, are used also with the dative.

ADVERBS.

§ **38.** **a.** *a.* A predicate adjective is often used where the English idiom has an adverb or an adverbial phrase, as χθιζὸς ἔβη A 424 *went yesterday,* ἠερίη A 497 *early in the morning,* πανημέριοι Α 472 *all day long*, παννύχιος a 443 *through the whole night*, μεταδόρπιος δ 194 *after supper*, ἐννύχιοι Λ 683 *by night*, ἔνδιοι Λ 726 *at midday*, ἑσπέριοι ξ 344 *at evening*, πρηνής Ε 58 (*pronus*) *on his face*, ἐπομφάλιον Η 267 (ἐπ᾽ ὀμφαλῷ) *on the boss*, δέξιον Κ 274 *on the right*, μετώπιον Π 739 *on the forehead*, πεζός Ω 438 *on foot*.

β. Similarly κεῖνος Ω 412 *there*, οὗτος Κ 341 *here*, and frequently ὅδε, as ἡμεῖς οἵδε a 76 *we here*.

γ. πρόφρων *willing* is used only predicatively, where the English idiom uses *willingly*.

b. Adverbs ending in -α are common: λίγα (but λιγέως is more frequent), σάφα, τάχα (about 70 times, but ταχέως only ψ 365), ὦκα. These seem to have been originally neuter cognate accusatives, and many are such still; *cf.* πόλλ᾽ ἐπέτελλε, πόλλ᾽ ἠρᾶτο, μέγα νήπιε, μεγάλ᾽ εὔχετο, κτλ.

c. Adverbs in -δην and -δον (originally adverbial accusatives from stems in -δα and -δο) are: ἀμβολάδην, βάδην, ἐπιγράβδην, ἐπιλίγδην, ἐπιστροφάδην, κλήδην, κρύβδην, μεταδρομάδην, ὀνομακλήδην, παραβλήδην, προτροπάδην, ὑποβλήδην (all having the signification of the participle of the corresponding verb), — ἀγεληδόν, ἀναφανδόν, ἀνα- (ἀπο-, ἐπι-, περι-) σταδόν, βοτρυδόν, διακριδόν, ἰλαδόν, καταφυλαδόν, κατωμαδόν, κλαγγηδόν, πανθυμαδόν, φαλαγγηδόν.

d. Adverbs in -δα are rare, as ἀναφανδά, ἀποσταδά, μίγδα.

e. Adverbs in -δις are: ἄλλυδις, ἀμοιβηδίς, ἄμυδις, ἀμφουδίς.

f. Adverbs in -ι are: ἀμογητί, ἀναιμωτί, ἀνιδρωτί, ἀνουτητί, ἀνωιστί, ἀσπουδί.

g. Adverbs in -ξ are: γνύξ, ἐπιμίξ, κουρίξ, λάξ, ὀδάξ, πύξ.

h. Adverbs in -ως are not common; they are most frequent from ο-stems: οὕτως (οὗτος), ὥς (ὅ), αὔτως (αὐτός), κακῶς (κακός). ἴσως and ὁμοίως are not found, καλῶς only β 63, φίλως only Δ 347.

Adverbs in -ως are formed also from ἀφραδής (ἀφραδέως) ἀσφαλής (ἀσφαλέως), λιγύς (λιγέως), μέγας (μεγάλως), ταχύς (ταχέως), τεχνήεις (τεχνηέντως), and from the participles (used like adjectives) ἐπιστάμενος, ἐσσύμενος.

These adverbs in -ως are little used also by the lyric poets: καλῶς, κακῶς, ἴσως, ἄλλως are not found in Pindar.

HOMERIC VERSE.

§ 39. The Heroic Hexameter. a. The poems are to be read with careful attention to the metrical quantity of each syllable, as well as to the sense of the passage. There are six feet (bars or measures) in each verse; hence the name *hexameter*. The part of each foot which has no ictus (the *arsis*) should receive as much time though not so much stress as the ictus-syllable (the *thesis*). The rhythm would be called $\frac{2}{4}$ time in modern music. The English hexameter (found *e.g.* in Longfellow's *Evangeline*) is generally read as of $\frac{3}{8}$ time.

b. The written word-accent is to be disregarded in reading Homeric verse. Occasionally (as ἄνδρα μοι ἔννεπε, μοῦσα, πολύτροπον ὃς μάλα πολλά a 1) the verse-ictus and word-accent may coincide, but the word-accent seems to have had no influence on the formation of the verse.

c. The dactyl (♩ ♪ ♪ or _ ∪ ∪), with the ictus on the first syllable, is the fundamental and prevailing foot of Homeric verse. It is often replaced by a spondee [1] or heavy dactyl (♩ ♩ or _ _). In three verses of the Iliad (B 544, Λ 130, Ψ 221) and in three of the Odyssey (o 334, φ 15, χ 192) each foot is a spondee, but a restoration of older, un-

---

[1] This name was derived from the use of this slow solemn measure in the hymns which accompanied the libation (σπονδή) to the gods; *cf.* two brief hymns of the Lesbian Terpander, about 700 B.C., to Zeus: Ζεῦ πάντων ἀρχά, | πάντων ἀγήτωρ, | Ζεῦ, σοὶ σπένδω | ταύταν ὕμνων ἀρχάν, and to Apollo and the Muses: Σπένδωμεν ταῖς Μνάμας | παισὶν Μώσαις | καὶ τῷ Μωσάρχῳ | Λατοῦς υἱεῖ.

contracted forms would give at least one dactyl to each of
these verses; Ἀτρείδης· τὼ δ᾽ αὖτ᾽ ἐκ δίφρου γουναζέσθην Λ
130 may be read with two dactyls Ἀτρείδης· τὼ δ᾽ αὖτ᾽ ἐκ
δίφροο (§ 17 c) γουναζέσθην.

Dactyls are about three times as frequent as spondees in
the Homeric poems.

d. Verses in which each of the first five feet is a dactyl
are far more common in Homer than in Vergil: there are
160 in the first book of the Iliad alone. Many frequently
recurring verses have this rhythm; as τὸν δ᾽ ἀπαμειβόμενος
προσέφη πόδας ὠκὺς Ἀχιλλεύς, — οἳ δ᾽ ἐπ᾽ ὀνείαθ᾽ ἑτοῖμα προ-
κείμενα χεῖρας ἴαλλον, — αὐτὰρ ἐπεὶ πόσιος καὶ ἐδητύος ἐξ
ἔρον ἕντο. Many other verses have but one spondee (generally in the first foot) among the first five feet; as ἦμος δ᾽
ἠριγένεια φάνη ῥοδοδάκτυλος ἠώς, — ἦμος δ᾽ ἠέλιος κατέδυ καὶ
ἐπὶ κνέφας ἦλθεν.

e. Spondees are most common in the first two feet; they
are more and more avoided in each foot toward the close of
the verse, except perhaps in the fourth foot where the great
Alexandrian critic Aristarchus preferred a spondee. But
very many of these spondees in the first and fourth feet of
our texts can be and doubtless should be resolved into dactyls; thus ἀγήραον B 447 is now read for the ἀγήρων of Aristarchus.

f. The first foot allows more freedom than any other. A
short vowel there more frequently retains its natural quantity before a mute and a liquid, and yet is more frequently
lengthened in the unaccented part of the foot (§ 41 h γ) before that combination. At the close of the first foot, hiatus
is allowed (§ 9 b).

Similarly the first foot of the iambic trimeter of Greek
tragedy and of English poetry has exceptional freedom.

g. The Bucolic diaeresis (§ 40 h) is seldom immediately
preceded by a word of three long syllables. Before this
diaeresis, a dactyl is strongly preferred, and is to be restored

in many places where the Mss. have the contracted form. Certain dactylic forms, as βήσετο, are preserved there more frequently than elsewhere in the verse.

h. Verses which have a spondee in the fifth foot are called spondaic verses (ἔπη σπονδειακά). They are more common in Homer than in the Latin poets, — about 4 *per cent.* of the verses of the Iliad being spondaic.

i. These spondaic verses seem especially frequent at the close of emphatic sentences or of divisions of the narrative (*cf.* A 21, 157, 291, 600) and in descriptions of suffering and toil, but often no rhythmic effect is sought; the convenience of the verse determined the measure.

j. The last two feet of the verse must not consist of two spondaic words: thus Ἡῶ δῖαν ι 306 should be Ἡόα δῖαν, δήμου φῆμις ξ 239 should be δήμοο φῆμις.

k. The last foot in each verse is a spondee, but the final syllable may be short; the deficiency in time is then made up by the slight pause which follows at the end of the verse (§ 41 *a, p a*). A heavy or consonantal ending is preferred; hence the ν-movable is often used.

l. The student need not concern himself about elision as in Latin poetry; that is already done in the text; but he must be watchful for synizesis (§ 7).

CAESURAL PAUSES.

§ **40.** **a.** Each verse has one or more caesural pauses (*caesura* = τομή *cutting*), — pauses within a foot.

b. The principal caesura of the verse is always a pause in the sense, and is often emphasized by punctuation, as in each of the six successive verses Ξ 10–15; but occasionally commas are found where no pause is necessary.

Of course there can be no pause immediately before an enclitic, since this is closely connected with the foregoing word.

c. A caesura is almost always found in the third foot;

only 185 verses of the Iliad and 71 of the Odyssey have no
pause there.   It occurs either after the ictus-syllable (as
μῆνιν ἄειδε θεά ∧ Πηληιάδεω ᾿Αχιλῆος A 1 _ ∪ ∪ | _ ∪ ∪ |
_ ∧ _ | _ ∪ ∪ | _ ∪ ∪ | _ _ |) or between the two short sylla-
bles (as ἄνδρα μοι ἔννεπε Μοῦσα ∧ πολύτροπον ὃς μάλα πολλά
a 1, _ ∪ ∪ | _ ∪ ∪ | _ ∪ ∧ ∪ | _ ∪ ∪ | _ ∪ ∪ | _ _ |).   These
two caesuras are about equally frequent; but the second
slightly predominates and seems to have been preferred.

   d. The importance of the caesura in the third foot is
marked not only by the freedom with which hiatus is allowed there (§ 9 b), and by the evident avoidance of elision
at that point (§ 10 e), but also by the large number of tags
of verses which are suited to follow it; as πατὴρ ἀνδρῶν τε
θεῶν τε, βοῶπις πότνια ῞Ηρη, θεὰ λευκώλενος ῞Ηρη, θεὰ γλαυκῶπις ᾿Αθήνη, φιλομμειδὴς ᾿Αφροδίτη, Διὸς θυγάτηρ ᾿Αφροδίτη,
ἐϋκνήμιδες ᾿Αχαιοί, ᾿Αχαιῶν χαλκοχιτώνων, κάρη κομόωντες
᾿Αχαιοί, ἀρηΐφιλος Μενέλαος, ἄναξ ἀνδρῶν ᾿Αγαμέμνων, βοὴν
ἀγαθὸς Διομήδης, Γερήνιος ἱππότα Νέστωρ, κτλ. — all of
which must be preceded by the feminine caesura (see f) of
the third foot; while ᾿Αγαμέμνονος ᾿Ατρείδαο, εὐρὺ κρείων
᾿Αγαμέμνων, ἡγήτορες ἠδὲ μέδοντες, ἀπαμείβετο φώνησέν τε
κτλ. must be preceded by the masculine caesura of the third
foot.   See § 4 b, c, d.

   e. The pause after the first syllable of the third foot is
called the *penthemimeral* caesura (πέντε, ἡμι-, μέρος) because
it comes after the fifth half-foot; it divides the verse into
2½ + 3½ feet.   The pause between the two short syllables of
the third foot divides the verse into 2¾ + 3¼ feet.

   f. The pause after an ictus-syllable is called a *masculine*
caesura because of the vigorous tone which it gives to the
verse; the pause between two unaccented syllables is called
a *feminine* caesura.

   g. Sometimes the principal pause of the verse is the masculine caesura of the fourth foot.   This is called the *hephthemimeral* caesura (ἑπτά, ἡμι-, μέρος).   This is somewhat more

common in the Iliad than in the Odyssey. It is frequent
after a feminine caesura of the third foot. It gives an ener-
getic movement after a penthemimeral caesura, when the
verse is divided into $2\frac{1}{2} + 1 + 2\frac{1}{2}$ feet.

h. Sometimes the pause of the verse is at the close of the
fourth foot; this is called the *Bucolic* diaeresis (a diaeresis
being a pause at the end of a word *between* two feet) or caesura, since it is most evidently aimed at in the bucolic or
pastoral poetry of Theocritus. Occasionally there is a transition at this point to another part of the story, as A 318,
348, 430. This Bucolic diaeresis with the penthemimeral
caesura divides the verse into $2\frac{1}{2} + 1\frac{1}{2} + 2$ feet.

i. The importance of the Bucolic diaeresis is marked by
the large number of tags of verses which are ready to follow
it, as δῖος Ὀδυσσεύς, ἕρκος Ἀχαιῶν, ἱππότα Νέστωρ, ὄβριμος
Ἄρης, φαίδιμος Ἕκτωρ, Φοῖβος Ἀπόλλων, Παλλὰς Ἀθήνη, δῖα
θεάων, μητίετα Ζεύς, ἰσόθεος φώς. See § 4 *c*. Hiatus is allowed here occasionally. See § 9 *b*.

j. A slight pause occurs after the first short syllable of the
first foot about 50 times in 100 verses.

k. A slight pause occurs about as often, after the first
short syllable of the fifth foot. The poet prefers to close the
verse with the rhythm $-\smile, \smile--$ (where the comma represents the end of a word) rather than $-\smile\smile, --$; hence οὔτε
τέλεσσας A 108, not οὔτ' ἐτέλεσσας. See § 25 *e*.

l. The principal pause of the verse is almost never at the
close of the third foot; this would divide the verse into two
equal parts and cause monotony. A word ends there not
infrequently, but is accompanied by a more prominent caesura in the third or fourth foot; as ἔνθα ἴδον πλείστους Φρύ-
γας ἄνερας Γ 185, where the last two words are so closely
connected that no caesura is felt between them. But see γ 34.

m. Even a slight pause is rare between the two short syllables of the fourth foot. In καὶ ἐπείθετο μυθῷ A 33, the
objectionable pause might be avoided by omitting the aug-

ment, but the conjunction is connected with the verb so closely that no caesura is felt.

n. It has been remarked that the forbidden caesura is next in position to the favorite Bucolic diaeresis; while the forbidden diaeresis at the close of the third foot is next to the favorite feminine caesura of the third foot.

o. No sentence ends with the second foot.

p. The pause in the third foot gives to the rest of the verse an anapaestic movement, from which it is often recalled by the Bucolic diaeresis. Similarly the Roman Saturnian verse (as *Dabúnt malúm Metélli* ∧ *Naévió poétae*) is at first iambic, but is trochaic at the close.

q. The varied position of the main caesura, and the minor pauses in different parts of the verse, give perfect freedom from monotony without detracting from the grace and dignity of the measure.

QUANTITY.[1]

§ 41. a. Metrical convenience or necessity often determined the poet's choice among synonymous words (§ 4 *a–d*); since ἀμφιδέξιος *ambidexter* was not suited to dactylic verse, περιδέξιος was used Φ 163. The poet in general preferred the light dactyls to the heavy dactyls or spondees, and retained

---

[1] The beginner will find it convenient to remember concerning α, ι, υ, the vowels whose quantity is not clear at the first glance, that

(1) they are short in the final syllable of any word when the antepenult has the acute or if the penult has the circumflex accent;

(2) they are regularly short in inflectional endings, as μάχῃσι, ἥρωα, τρέπουσι, τέθνηκα, — in the final syllables of neuter nouns, as δῶμα, ἦμαρ, μέλι, δάκρυ, — in suffixes, except where ν has been lost before σ, as φύσϊς, δολίης, Φοίνισσα, — in particles, especially in prepositions, as ἀνά, περί, ὑπό, ἄρα, ἔτι, — and generally in the second aorist stem of verbs;

(3) they are long in the final syllable when the penult is long by nature and has the acute accent;

(4) they are long when they are the result of contraction, as ἐτίμᾱ from ἐτίμαε, ἱρόν from ἱερόν, νέκῡς from νέκυας, and as the final vowel of the stem of nouns of the first declension.

in the Epic dialect a large number of dactylic forms which
were afterwards contracted. An *amphimacer* (_ ◡ _, ἀμφί,
μακρόν) was avoided often by means of apocope, synizesis, or
elision.

Most exceptions to the rules of quantity are only apparent.
The poet, for example, did not lengthen a short syllable by
placing the ictus upon it. If an apparently short final syllable stands where a long syllable is expected, it is probable
either

(1) that the final syllable was originally long, and later
lost part of its quantity, as πρίν, nouns in -ις (βλοσυρῶπις
ἐστεφάνωτο Λ 36), and the dative singular ending of the
third declension (§ 18 *a*); or

(2) that the following word has lost an initial consonant
which would have made the preceding syllable long by position (see *m* below); or

(3) that the pause (musical *rest*) of a caesura or diaeresis,
fills out the time occupied by the foot, allowing the same
freedom as at the end of the verse (§ 39 *k*).

b. A considerable number of anomalies, however, remain
unexplained. Prominent among the unexplained anomalies
of quantity is the ῑ of certain abstract nouns, as ὑπεροπλίῃσι
Α 205, προθυμίῃσι Β 588, ἀτιμίῃσι ν 142. This ι receives no
ictus, hence no satisfaction could be gained even from the
obsolete doctrine that a short syllable might be lengthened
by the poet if it were made the ictus-syllable of the foot.
These abstract nouns form such a definite class that it may
be assumed that there was some explanation, perhaps physio-
logical, for them all.

c. Doubtless when the poems were recited musically, it
might have been easy for the bard in his intonation to hold,
and thus to lengthen, a syllable which was usually short, or
to slur over a long syllable and treat it as short. But it is
not found that Homer or any other poet availed himself of
this license.

d. Many apparently irregular variations of natural quantity, as well as apparent freedom in allowing hiatus, and variations of quantity made by position (see *m* below), are to be
explained by the loss of a consonant, *e.g.* ἄτη or ἀάτη was
originally ἀϝατη (see § 14 *j*); the loss of ϝ and the conse-
quent lengthening of one of the neighboring vowels (*cf.*
βασιλεϝος, βασιλῆος, βασιλέως), explains ἀασάμην I 116 and
ἀάσατο I 537, as compared with ἄασας Θ 237; ἄεσαμεν (ἀϝε-
σαμεν, from ἰαύω) γ 151 but ἄεσαν γ 490; ᾽Αϊδος Γ 322 but
᾽Αϊδι A 3, from α-ϝιδ (§ 14), *cf.* ἠείδης X 280 for ἐϝείδης;
μέμασαν B 863 but μεμαότες B 818 (μεμαϝοτες). In εὔκηλος
A 554 (ἔκηλοι E 759), the form may have been favored in
popular use by a supposed connection with the adverb εὖ,
which seemed so natural in εὔαδεν Ξ 340 for ἐϝαδεν.

e. It may be supposed that the bards followed poetic prece-
dents in allowing hiatus or lengthening before certain syllables in which but a minimum of the original sound remained;
sometimes, by false analogy, they may have treated in the
same way other syllables which really had lost no consonant.

f. *a.* A syllable which contains a long vowel or a diphthong is long by *nature*. Final αι and οι are metrically long,
although short as concerns accentuation.

β. The quantity of some vowels is not fixed, as ᾽Απόλλω-
νος A 14, ᾽Απόλλων A 380; ῎Αρες, ῎Αρες E 31 (if the text is
right); Σῑδόνες Ψ 743, Σῑδονίους δ 84; *cf.* Διονύσου λ 325
with Διώνυσος Z 135 (which remained the usual form in
Boeotian dialect, as it is in Pindar); ὕδωρ α 110, ὕδωρ α 146.

γ. Most of these vowels with variable quantity were originally long and were becoming short, as the Homeric ἶσος,
κᾱλός, and φᾱρος, became ἴσος, καλός, and φάρος in Attic
poetry. The penult of ἀνίη was long in Homer but occasionally short in Attic poetry. ϝειαρινό (*cf.* ὥρῃ εἰαρινῇ B
471), Attic ἐαρινός, is found on a Boeotian inscription. It
is evident that every vowel which at first was long and afterwards became short must have had at some time a metrical

quantity which could be treated either as long or short, *i.e.* its quantity was variable.

δ. A trace of the original ā in the ending of the neuter plural remains perhaps in ἔθνεα εἶσι B 87, where the hiatus is justified as *weak* (§ 9 *d*).

ε. For the length of final ι in the dative singular of the third declension, see § 18 *a*. πρίν in πρὶν αὖτ' Z 81 retains its original length, as a contracted comparative.

ζ. So in Latin, the vowels of certain words had lost so much of their original quantity in the time of Plautus that he employed them sometimes as long, sometimes as short, while in later Latin poetry they became definitely short. Analogous to this, also, is the fact that a short vowel before a mute and a liquid is generally long in Homer, while in Attic it is generally short.

η. With this variation of natural quantity may be compared the double forms employed in Homer, — one with a single consonant, another with two consonants, as Ἀχιλλεύς A 54, Ἀχιλεύς A 199; Ὀδυσσεύς A 430, Ὀδυσεύς Δ 494; Τρίκκην B 729, Τρίκης Δ 202; ὅππως A 344, ὅπως A 136; μέσσον Γ 266, μέσον A 481, κτλ., many of which doubled consonants are known to be justified etymologically.

g. Sometimes a naturally short vowel was lengthened (not by the poet, but in the speech of the people) in order to avoid the too frequent recurrence of short syllables. This is illustrated by the rule for the use of ο or ω in the comparison of adjectives (σοφώτερος but κουφότερος), by the pains shown by some of the Greek orators (as Demosthenes) to avoid an uninterrupted succession of several short syllables, and by the words which have a vowel similarly lengthened in the Attic dialect (as ἀθάνατος, προσήγορος, ὑπηρέτης). We find ἀνήρ but ἀνέρες (ἀνήρ M 382), *cf.* ἠνορέη (Pindar ἀνήρ, ἀνορέα) Πρίαμος but Πριαμίδης, θυγάτηρ but θυγάτερα (with ῡ in all forms of more than three syllables), ἀπονέοντο, ἀγοράασθε but ἀγορή, ἀθάνατος but ἄθαπτος, *cf.* ἠνεμόεντα from ἄνεμος, ἐπίτονος μ 423.

h. *a.* In Homeric verse a syllable which contains a short vowel is long by *position* when the vowel is followed by a double consonant (ζ, ξ, ψ) or by two or more consonants, whether these are in the same or in the following word or are divided between the two words.

β. This rule holds good also in case of a mute followed by a liquid. This combination rarely fails to make position within a word, and generally makes position when it stands at the beginning of a word (as ὕπατε κρειόντων a 45), especially when this word is closely connected with the preceding.

γ. The influence of the metrical ictus on quantity is nowhere else so clear as in strengthening this so-called *weak-position* before a mute and a liquid: before this combination, a short vowel is always lengthened (more than 2600 times) in the ictus part of the foot; while lengthening of an ultima in the arsis is found 105 times, 48 of which are in the first foot (as ἐκ δὲ Χρυσηίς A 439, *cf.* § 39*f*) and 47 in the second foot (as ἐξ οὗ δὴ τὰ πρῶτα A 6). Of course a short vowel remains short only in the unaccented part of the foot. See *i* β below.

i. *a.* Sometimes a vowel remains short before a mute followed by λ or ρ, as Ἀφροδίτη Γ 380, ἀμφῐβρότης B 389, ἀμφῐ-δρυφής B 700, πρὸτραπέσθαι Z 336, νεῦσὲ Κρονίων A 528, βάλὲ Πριαμίδαο Γ 356, γάρ ῥᾰ Κλῠταιμνήστρης A 113. These words and phrases could not have been brought into the verse if the mute and liquid must make position, and the history of the language shows that this combination of mute and liquid was losing its weight (*cf. f* γ above). Similarly, the syllable must be short which precedes βροτῶν, προσηύδα, τράπεζα.

β. Of about 570 examples in the Homeric poems of a vowel remaining short before initial mute and liquid, it is said that 202 are in the first short syllable of the third foot (as ὣς οἳ μὲν τοιαῦτα πρὸς ἀλλήλους ἀγόρευον E 274), 278 are in the first short syllable of the fifth foot (as καί μιν φωνήσας

ἔπεα πτερόεντα προσηύδα Α 201), 28 are in the first short syllable of the first foot (as ἦκα πρὸς ἀλλήλους Γ 155), 27 are
in the first short syllable of the second foot (as ὡς δ' ὅτε τίς
τε δράκοντα Γ 33) ; while only 34 are in the second short syllable of a dactyl, 25 of these being in the first foot (as καὶ
βάλε Πριαμίδαο Γ 356), and only one of the 34 being before
a sonant mute followed by a liquid (τὰ δὲ δράγματα Λ 69).
It is evident that the numbers in such computations differ
with different texts.

γ. That a mute and liquid do not always make position
is explained by the ease with which the combination can be
pronounced at the beginning of a syllable, leaving the preceding vowel short.

δ. In ἀνδροτῆτα Ω 6, *a* remains short before three consonants; but it is probable that this word has replaced some
obsolete synonymous word which suited the metre.

ε. Before four words, two of which begin with the double
consonant ζ and two with the two consonants σκ (not a mute
and a liquid), the preceding vowel remains short: οἵ τε Ζά-
κυνθον Β 634, οἳ δὲ Ζέλειαν Β 824, προχέοντο Σκαμάνδριον Β
465, ἔπειτα σκέπαρνον ε 237. Two of these words, Ζάκυνθος
and Σκάμανδρος (although the gods called it Ξάνθος, Υ 74),
might seem essential to the poet's story, and might be ex-
cused by the greater freedom which is allowed to the treatment of proper names in verse; but there are indications of
possible collateral forms with a single consonant; *cf.* κίδνα-
μαι with σκίδναμαι (which is always used where the metre
permits), μικρός with σμικρός (§ 12 *j*). Perhaps Δάκυνθος
should be substituted for Ζάκυνθος, *cf.* ζαθέην Α 38 with
δαφοινός Β 308, Δεύξιππος in a Boeotian inscription for Ζεύ-
ξιππος, Δάγλη on coins for Ζάγκλη. It is noteworthy, however, that Ζάκυνθος was also the Greek name of Saguntum
and in that word Ζ may often have been pronounced nearly
like Σ.

j. *a.* A single λ, μ, ν, ρ, σ, at the beginning of certain

words, may make position (*cf.* § 12 *b*): πολλὰ λισσομένω
Χ 91 _ _ | _ ◡ ◡ | _ (*cf.* ἐλλίσσετο Ζ 45, τρίλλιστος Θ 488,
πολύλλιστον ε 445, οὐδὲ κατὰ μοῖραν Π 367 (*cf.* ἄμμορον Ζ
408, διεμοιρᾶτο ξ 434, ἔμμορε Α 278, εἵμαρτο ε 312, of which
the form of reduplication indicates that the stem was treated
as if it began with two consonants, § 25 *o*), ἔπεα νιφάδεσσι
Γ 222 (*cf.* ἀγά-ννιφον Α 420 and English *snow*), ὅσα ῥέζεσκον
χ 46 (*cf.* ϝέργον, *work*, *wrought*), ὕλη τε σεύαιτο Ψ 198 (*cf.*
ἐσσεύοντο Β 808, ἐπισσεύεσθαι Ο 347, λαοσσόος Ν 128).

β. So also δ makes position in the stem δι- (δεῖσαι *fear*)
and always in δήν *long*, as ἡμεῖς δὲ δείσαντες ι 236, ἔδεισεν δ᾽ ὁ
γέρων Α 33, *cf.* θεουδής ζ 121 *god-fearing* (for θεο-δϝης); οὔ
τι μάλᾱ δήν Α 416.

γ. A short vowel before a liquid is lengthened most frequently when it is in the ictus-syllable of the second or
fourth foot (seldom in the third or fifth foot) and generally
before words which begin with two short syllables, as ἐνὶ
μεγάροισι γενέθλη Ε 270.

k. It is stated that a short vowel is lengthened 123 times
before ρ (91 times, not counting repetitions), 70 (51) times
before λ, 320 (111) times before μ, 58 (30) times before ν,
44 (29) times before δ, 9 times before σ.

l. *a.* Cognate languages and collateral dialectic forms
show that most words which in the Attic dialect began with
ρ, once began with σρ or ϝρ. This explains the doubling of
the ρ after the augment and in composition, as well as its
power to make position in Homeric verse. 85 *per cent.* of
the instances of lengthening before ρ are known to be justified etymologically.

β. The stem of the verb δεῖσαι is found on a Corinthian
inscription as δϝι. In the Homeric time, if the ϝ was not
still pronounced by the Ionians of Asia Minor, doubtless the
δ was thickened in pronunciation by the disappearing ϝ.

γ. Of the instances of lengthening before μ, most are only
physiologically explained; the μ-sound being easily continued

until it is virtually a double consonant; but this lengthening
occurs only before certain stems, not before μάχεσθαι, μένειν,
μοῦνος κτλ.

m. One of the consonants which made position has often
been lost, as γρηὶ δέ μιν Ϝεϊκυῖα Γ 386, πάρειπών Λ 793 (παρ-
Ϝειπών, § 14); βέλος ἐχεπευκές A 51, γὰρ ἔχον Τ 49, πᾶρ-
έχῃ τ 113, from the stem σεχ-, *cf.* σῦνεχές ι 74 (for συνσε-
χες); θεὸς ὥς Γ 230 (for θεὸς ϳώς, § 12 *l*), *cf.* κακὸν ὥς Β 190,
ὄρνιθες ὥς Γ 2, πέλεκυς ὥς Γ 60, οἱ δ' ἄρ' ἴσαν ὡς εἴ τε Β 780.
Both consonants which made position are occasionally lost,
especially in the stem of the third personal pronoun (§ 14 *c*, *h*),
as ἄρᾱ ᾧ Ρ 196 for ἄρα σϜῷ, ἀπὸ ἔο Τ 261 for ἀπὸ σϜέο. But
see § 14 *j*.

n. φ seems to be used as a double consonant in Ζεφυρίη
η 119 _ ∪ ∪ _, ὄφιν Μ 208 _ ∪, πιφαύσκω Κ 478 (although
here the reduplication πι may be considered long by nature,
cf. Σίσυφος Ζ 154). ὄπφις is now written for ὄφις in Hip-
ponax Frg. 49, and is justified etymologically; *cf.* Σάπφω
from the stem of σοφός, Ἴακχος from ἰάχω, ὄκχον (ὄχον) Pindar *Ol.* VI 24, φαιὄχιτωνες Aesch. *Choeph.* 1047.

o. *a.* A long final vowel or diphthong in the arsis of the
foot is shortened before a following vowel: Ἀτρεΐδαι τε καὶ
ἄλλοι ἐυκνήμιδες Ἀχαιοί A 17, τὴν δ' ἐγὼ οὐ λύσω Α 29. The
shortening of a long vowel is essentially the elision of half
the vowel (§ 9 *d*).

β. The most frequent exceptions to this rule occur in the
first foot, less often in the fourth foot, — before the diaereses
where hiatus is most common (§ 9 *b*).

γ. Final αι, οι, ει are most frequently shortened before an
initial vowel. Final οι is shortened eight times as often as
final η.

δ. The diphthongs with υ seem to have been more firm in
retaining their quantity than those with ι. This is explained
perhaps by the greater permanence in the language of Ϝ over ϳ.

ε. This shortening of diphthongs seems to indicate a ten-

dency of the final ι or υ of the diphthong to go into its cognate y (j) or w (ϝ) sound and disappear (cf. § 5 g). In
Pindar, also, a final diphthong is shortened far oftener (five
times as often) than a long final vowel. Of course there was
no hiatus as long as the j or ϝ was spoken.

ζ. Final ῳ and η are shortened before an initial vowel more
rarely than other diphthongs. η, ῃ, ω, ῳ, ευ are shortened
more frequently than elsewhere when they are in the first
short syllable of the first foot. ῳ is seldom shortened except
before an ε or (less frequently) an α.

p. α. Before a pause (as before the close of the verse, see
§ 39 k), a short vowel may be used in place of a long vowel:
ἐκπέρσαι Πριάμοιο πόλιν Α 19 — — | — ∪ ∪ | — ∪ ∪ | ≃ ∧, φεύ-
γωμεν· ἔτι γὰρ κτλ. κ 269 — — | ∪ ∧ ∪ ∪ | —, εἵατ᾽ ἀκούοντες·
ὁ κτλ. α 326 — ∪ ∪ | — — | ∪ ∧. Not infrequently thus the
short final vowel of a vocative takes the place of a long syllable, even ὦ υἱὲ Πετεῶο Δ 338; in such cases the nominative
form frequently could be used. The pause in the rhythm
occupies the remainder of the time which would be spent in
pronouncing a long syllable, ♪♩ ♩ = ♩ ♩. Before a pause,
also, a long final vowel may preserve its quantity although
the following word begins with a vowel.

β. This pause, which allows hiatus and prevents the shortening of a final vowel, gives prominence to the syllable before
it, as ἐκ γὰρ Ὀρέσταο ∧ τίσις ἔσσεται α 40, οἳ μὲν δυσομένου ∧
Ὑπερίονος α 24.

q. A few verses seem to begin with a short syllable, as
ἐπειδὴ τὸ πρῶτον δ 13 (probably ἐπϝει), φίλε κασίγνητε Φ 308
(cf. φίλαι Ε 117, ἐφίλατο Ε 61), ὃς ἄξει Ω 154 (for ὅς ϝ ἄξει =
ὅς ϝε ἄξει, cf. ὅς σ᾽ ἄξει Ω 183), ὃς ἤδη τά τ᾽ ἐόντα Α 70 (for
ὃς ϝείδη, § 14), ἀείδη ρ 519 for ἀϝείδη (see d above); βορέης
Ι 5 is in all Mss. for βορρῆς (Thuc. VI 2). For Ζεφυρίη η
119, see n above; for συνεχές Μ 26, see m above; for ἐπίτονος, see g above; but διὰ μὲν ἀσπίδος Γ 357 seems to have
been used on the analogy of δῐ᾽ Ἀφροδίτη κτλ.

GREEK INDEX.

Ἀτρείδης, 57 f.
Ἀτρείων, 59.
ἀτρέμα, 45.
Αὐγηιάδαο, 57.
αὐέρυσαν, 42.
αὐίαχοι, 48.
αὐτάρ, 32.
αὐτόθεν, 50.
αὐτός, 63.
αὐτόφι, 50.
αὔτως, 63.
ἀφίει, 65.
Ἀχαιίδες, 58.
Ἀχιλεύς, 89.
βάλλεο, 69.
βάρδιστος, 59.
βασιλεύτερος, 60.
βασιλῆος, 38.
βεβαῶτα, 68.
βεβήκειν, 67.
βεβλήκειν, 45.
βείομαι, 73.
βελέεσσι, 52.
βέομαι, 73.
βήσεο, 73.
βίη Ἡρακληείη, 21, 54.
βλῆτο, 77.
βόλεται, 38.
Βορέω, 51.
βοῦς ταῦρος, 14.
Βρισηίδα, 58.
βροτός, 44.
γαιήοχος, 12.
γαλόῳ, 52.
γάστρην, 55.
γέ, 29.
γέλως, 53.
γενοίατο, 69.
γέντο, 77.
γέρα, 53.
γῆ, 35.
γηθῆσαι, 68.
γηράς, 77.
γλαυκώπιδα, 53.

γλαυκῶπις, 12.
γνώωσι, 76.
δαήσεαι, 75.
δαινύατο, 70.
δαινῦτο, 70.
δακρυόφι, 49.
δαμάᾳ, 72.
δαμεῖεν, 66.
Δαρδανίδης, 59.
Δαρδανίδων, 58.
Δαρδανίωνες, 58.
δαφοινός, 91.
δέ in apodosis, 30.
-δε, 50.
δεδαίαται, 69.
δειδέχαται, 67.
δείδια, 67.
δείδοικα, 67.
δείους, 54.
δεῖπνον, 22.
δεῖσαι, 92.
δέκτο, 77.
δέξιον, 80.
Δευκαλίδης, 58 f.
δεύτατος, 61.
δέχαται, 66.
δή, 29.
δὴ αὖτε, 39.
δήεις, 73.
δηιόῳεν, 72.
δηλήσηται, 70.
δήμου φῆμις, 83.
δήν, 92.
διαρραίσεσθαι, 74.
διδοῦναι, 68, 75.
διδοῦσι, 75.
διδώσω, 75.
διεμοιρᾶτο, 92.
διέτμαγεν, 70.
διίφιλος, 52.
διχθά, 44.
διώκετον, 67.
Διώνυσος, 88.
δοιοί κτλ., 61.

δούλιον ἦμαρ, 21.
δύη, 70.
δύσετο, 73.
δυσκλέα, 53.
δυσομένοιο, 73.
δῶσι, 67.
ἔ κτλ., 46.
ἐάγη, 66.
ἑάλην, 66.
ἔαρ, 46.
ἔασκες, 78.
ἔαται, 77.
ἔβαν, 70.
ἐβήσετο, 74.
ἔβλαβεν, 75.
ἐγδούπησαν, 44.
ἐγρήγορθε, 73.
ἐγχείη, 55.
ἔγχος, 22.
ἔδεισεν, 92.
ἔδνα, 46.
ἔδρακον, 45.
ἐδύσετο, 74.
ἐείκοσι, 49.
ἐέλδωρ, 49.
ἐέλπετο, 66.
ἔηκε, 66.
ἐήνδανε, 36, 66.
ἐῆος, 56.
ἔης, 64.
ἔθεν, 50, 62.
ἔθνος, 46.
εἰαρινῇ, 88.
εἴατο, 77.
εἶδον, 66.
εἴκοσι, 46.
ἐικυῖα, 74.
εἴκω, 46.
εἴμαρτο, 92.
εἰν, 79.
εἶναι κτλ., 34.
εἰνί, 79.
εἷο, 62.
εἷος, 37.

πολλός, 57.
πολύλλιστον, 92.
ποντοπορούσης, 39.
ποντόφι, 49.
ποσσί, 37, 43.
ποτί, 79.
πουλύς, 38, 57.
πρέσβα, 57.
πρηνής, 80.
Πρῖαμίδης, 89.
πρίν, 89.
προβλώσκειν, 44.
προθυμίῃσι, 87.
προσαυδήτην, 71.
προσώπατα, 53.
προτί, 79.
προύφαινε, 40.
προύχοντο, 40.
πρόφρασσα, 57.
πρόφρων, 80.
πρώτιστος, 60.
πτολεμίξομεν, 73.
πτόλεμος, 44.
πτόλις, 44.
πυλέων, 51.
πωλέαι, 72.
ῥά, 29.
ῥάσσατε, 69.
ῥερυπωμένα, 67.
ῥίπτασκε, 78.
σάω, 71.
σέθεν, 50 ; σεῖο, 62 f.
Σειρήνοιιν, 52.
Σκάμανδρος, 91.
Σμινθεῦ, 58.
σπεῖο, 71.
σπείους, 37.
σπέσσι, 52.
σπήεσσι, 54.
στήθεσφιν, 50.
σῦνεχές, 93.
συὸς κάπρου, 14.
σφέ, 62.
σῶμα, 23.

τ', 41.
Ταλαϊονίδαο, 59.
ταλαύρινον, 48.
τἆλλα, 40.
ταχέως, 81.
τέ, 29.
τέθναθι, 68.
τεθνηῶτος, 68.
Τελαμωνιάδης, 59.
Τελαμώνιος, 59.
τεοῖο, 62.
τεοῖσι, 65.
τερπικέραυνος, 45.
τέτλαθι, 68.
τετράφατο, 69.
τετύκοντο, 66.
τεῦ, 65.
τεχνηέντως, 81.
τεχνήσσαι, 39.
τέων, 65.
τιθεῖ, τιθήμενος, 75.
τίθημι, 23.
τιμῆς, 39.
τίσειαν, 68.
τοί, ταί, κτλ., 64.
τοίσδεσιν, 64.
τοίσδεσσιν, 64.
τοῖσι δ' ἀνέστη, 27.
τούνεκα, 40.
τραπείομεν, 45, 75.
τράφεν, 70.
τρίλλιστος, 92.
τριχθά, 44.
Τρωιάδων, 58.
Τυδῆ, 39.
τύνη, 62.
ὑββάλλειν, 42.
υἷες Ἀχαιῶν, 12.
υἱός, υἷος, κτλ., 55.
ὑμείων, 62.
ὔμμες, κτλ., 63.
ὑμός κτλ., 62 f.
ὑπαί, 79.
ὔπαιθα, 35, 50.

ὑπείρ, 79.
ὑπερδέα, 53.
Ὑπεριονίδαο, 59.
ὑπεροπλίῃσι, 87.
ὑπνώοντας, 72.
φάανθεν, 70, 75.
φαάντατος, 60.
φάνεσκε, 78.
φάο, 76.
φᾶρος, 23, 88.
φευγόντων, 68.
φηρσίν, 36.
φθῆσιν, 67.
φθίμην, φθῖτο, 70.
-φι, 49.
φιλεῦντας, 39.
φιλήμεναι, 72.
φλίψεται, 36.
φόβος, 23.
φορῆναι, 72.
φόως, 37.
φύγαδε, 50.
φύζα, 23.
φυλακούς, 55.
χαλκοχιτώνων, 12.
χαμαιευνάδες, 38.
χείρ, 38.
χἠμεῖς, 40.
χθιζός, 79.
χρεώ, 40.
χρή κτλ., 28.
Χρυσηίδα, 58.
ὦ ἀρίγνωτε, 40.
ὠδύσαο, 69.
ὤθεσκε, 78.
ὤκιστος, 59.
ὠκυρόῳ, 43.
ὤριστος, 40.
ὦρορε, 74 ; ὦρσε, 73.
ὡς (postpositive), 44.
ὧς, 64.
ὧς δ' αὔτως, 64.
ὥστε with inf., 26.
ωὗτος, 40.

INDEX OF SUBJECTS.

[The references are to pages.]

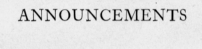

ANNOUNCEMENTS

COLLEGE SERIES OF
GREEK AUTHORS

Prepared under the supervision of JOHN WILLIAMS WHITE, THOMAS D.
SEYMOUR, and CHARLES BURTON GULICK

Books edited for college classes, with scholarly introductions, commentaries,
notes at the foot of each page, and vocabularies

Æschines against Ctesiphon (Richardson) $1.40
Æschylus: Prometheus Bound (Wecklein and Allen) 1.40
Aristophanes: Clouds (Humphreys) 1.40
Euripides: Bacchantes (Beckwith) 1.25
Euripides: Hippolytus (Harry) 1.40
Euripides: Iphigenia among the Taurians (Flagg) 1.40
Greek Dialects, Introduction to the Study of (Buck) 2.75
Homer: Iliad, Books I–III (Seymour) 1.40
Homer: Iliad, Books IV–VI (Seymour) 1.40
Homer: Iliad, Books XIX–XXIV (Clapp) 1.75
Homer: Odyssey, Books I–IV (Perrin) 1.40
Homer: Odyssey, Books V–VIII (Perrin) 1.40
Homer, Introduction to Language and Verse of (Seymour) . . .75
Lucian: Selected Writings (Allinson) 1.40
Lysias: Eight Orations (Morgan) 1.40
Menander: Four Plays (Capps) 2.50
Pausanias: Attica (Carroll) 1.65
Plato: Apology of Socrates, and Crito (Dyer and Seymour) . . 1.50
Plato: Gorgias (Lodge) 1.65
Plato: Protagoras (Towle) 1.25
Septuagint, Selections (Conybeare and Stock) 1.65
Sophocles: Antigone (D'Ooge) 1.40
Thucydides: Book I (Morris) 1.65
Thucydides: Book III (Smith) 1.65
Thucydides: Book V (Fowler) 1.40
Thucydides: Book VI (Smith) 1.50
Thucydides: Book VII (Smith) 1.40
Xenophon: Hellenica, Books I–IV (Manatt) 1.65
Xenophon: Hellenica, Books V–VII (Bennett) 1.40
Xenophon: Memorabilia (Smith) 1.40

Text editions of any of the above volumes, 40 cents each

GINN AND COMPANY PUBLISHERS

THE
ESSENTIALS OF LATIN SYNTAX

By CHARLES CHRISTOPHER MIEROW, Instructor in Classics
in Princeton University

12mo, cloth, 98 pages, 90 cents

THE first part of this book aims to present very clearly and concisely the essential facts of Latin syntax in compact and orderly form, and every construction named is so treated that its relation to Latin grammar in general is immediately apparent.

Each grammatical principle is illustrated by one simple and pertinent English example with its Latin equivalent, and with each instance there are references to the grammars of Allen and Greenough, West, and Bennett.

The second part consists of two sets of exercises for Latin writing, the one derived from Cæsar and the other from Livy; and each separate exercise, while based on some particular continuous portion of the text, illustrates at the same time some definite set of grammatical constructions already explained in the first part of the book.

As a review of grammar, "Essentials of Latin Syntax" is particularly useful in presenting the chief principles of syntax in simple tabular form. The Noun, the Pronoun, and the Verb are treated separately. A full index renders it an easy matter to refer to any construction.

THE
ESSENTIALS OF GREEK SYNTAX

By CHARLES CHRISTOPHER MIEROW, Instructor in Classics
in Princeton University

12mo, cloth, 165 pages, $1.25

PART FIRST consists of an outline of Greek syntax as an organized whole. The various constructions are arranged in simple tabular form, and each separate grammatical principle is illustrated by an English example with its equivalent in Greek. References to four Greek grammars are given in every case. In the treatment of the verb, especial attention is paid to conditional and relative conditional sentences and to indirect discourse.

Part Second consists of two groups of exercises for translation into Greek, each group containing four separate sets of exercises. The first group is intended for advanced classes in preparatory schools and is based on the Anabasis; the second, consisting of exercises to accompany Lysias and Plato's Apology, is designed for use with college freshmen.

The book contains very complete English and Greek indexes to facilitate reference to any construction.

GINN AND COMPANY PUBLISHERS